We Didn't Have Much,
But We Sure Had Plenty

Sherry Thomas is the coauthor
of *Country Women*

We Didn't Have Much, But We Sure Had Plenty

Stories of Rural Women

by Sherry Thomas

Illustrations by Judith A. Brown

ANCHOR BOOKS
ANCHOR PRESS/DOUBLEDAY
GARDEN CITY, NEW YORK
1981

This paperback edition is the first publication of *We Didn't Have Much, But We Sure Had Plenty.*
Anchor Books edition: 1981

Library of Congress Cataloging in Publication Data
Thomas, Sherry.
   We didn't have much, but we sure had plenty.
   1. Rural women—United States—Biography.
2. Farm life—United States. I. Title.
HQ1420.T56   305.4'3
ISBN: 0-385-14951-4
Library of Congress Catalog Card Number 80–956

For Carol, with love

My grateful thanks to everyone,
all across the country, who helped
me create this book

Contents

IV LOOKING AHEAD

Introduction

This book first began ten years ago, when a friend gave me a collection of Dorothea Lange's photographs of American country women. As I looked and looked at those photographs, studying their minute eloquent details, I wanted to hear those women speak, to know their stories. That was the beginning of what evolved this last year into a long trip zigzagging across the United States (seventeen thousand miles in all), looking for very ordinary women, meeting them, and asking about their lives.

In the intervening years, I had struggled to build a successful sheep ranch on a hundred-acre California coastal farm, had helped start a magazine for country women, and had coauthored the book *Country Women,* a practical guide for would-be farmers. Through all those years I had had over and over again to take great leaps of faith: to master skills that had been inconceivable to me, to live with my own internal hesitations, sometimes to become what I dreamed even before I was ready. Those were intoxicating years for me and the women around me, as we re-created ourselves in our own images, broke out of constraints that seemed to us generations old. We tried out "men's work," found our bodies and minds and spirits suited to it; found that we did not become men, but were instead strong women.

And all the while that I seemed to be living in the midst of a vibrant new women's culture, I felt something else pulling at me. I didn't want to throw away the past without understanding it. There were times, as when I organized neighborhood Fourth of July picnics or tried to explain responsibility to my hippie neighbors whose free-running dogs killed my sheep, that I felt personally anachronistic. I found age-old values and morals rising up in me, and proving personally important though they had little place in the counterculture around me. But more than that, I wanted to know about the women who had come before me. I wanted to know what they had done, what they had thought, what they had felt. And I became increasingly convinced that to ask the wrong questions was to get no answer at all. To know that she was so and so's wife or so and so's mother was a statement of her situation, but not of her experience.

And so, a year and a half ago, after two severe dog attacks had decimated my sheep flock and crippled my farm, it seemed a good time to take a look at America, to ponder the state of farms and farming, of communities and families, of traditional women's lives.

I put ads in rural magazines and spread the word to everyone I could, even friends of friends of friends, asking everywhere, "Did anyone have a relative, a neighbor, an acquaintance who was an older woman living on a farm?" Responses literally poured in and I sifted through them, trying to balance types of farms, geographic regions, economic status, racial and ethnic background: looking for as broad an American cross section as I could find.

The resulting trip, ten thousand miles one way across America to towns so tiny they appeared only on large-scale Census maps, caused untold headaches for the woman at AAA who worked out my route. "What do you want to go *there* for?" she asked.

But for me, the real question was how anyone too shy to order a hamburger in a small-town café could ever *interview* dozens of strangers. As nervous as I was, however, the trip was both an adventure and a sort of personal quest. I went wanting to understand the values on which people base their lives, wanting to record a way of life that is rapidly vanishing, wanting to know what women have done. And in the process of asking I found, if not answers, at least visions, images, simple phrases that resonated in my ears for days. This book grows out of a unique convergence: my own interest and the almost astonishing willingness of older women to speak deeply and honestly to a much younger stranger from California.

I interviewed fifty-six women on that first trip across the country, using a tape recorder to record our conversations. As I traveled I learned more and more about asking questions, and about listening with attentiveness. I found recurring themes and responses rising up to surprise me. I rapidly abandoned my preconceived questions and discovered instead that my task was to elicit someone else's story; to reach sometimes past memory back to the reality she had known.

From the first interviews in New Mexico to the last in Georgia, I struggled to understand a way of life that was so fundamentally different from what I had known. Where what you needed to live was raised or made, but rarely bought. Where money was sometimes nearly nonexistent. I had long been aware that the back-to-the-land movement's "simplicity" had its own brand of consumerism. But when Jaunita Sultemeier first told me about her family living on forty-five dollars a month in 1942, all of my rapid calculations to adjust for inflation didn't leave me with a 1940s version of today. Things were fundamentally different when they were produced not bought; the materialism to which we are all now so accustomed is a very recent phenomenon. There is a kind of personal power that comes from providing for oneself, from seeing the fruits of your actions, from knowing deeply that each thing that you do is part of a web of survival, from feeling linked to the earth, the seasons, your own body.

But that way of life was never romantic or easy. "I can't tell you what it took just to get a little butter," Gladys Sampson says. And she can't. From raising the feed for the cow to setting the butter molds in the spring box, it was a long, complicated, arduous process, as was every other daily task.

But for all the labor, another theme that came clear was that most people had lived satisfying lives. "We were *happier* then; we were truly happy people," I heard over and over. "We didn't have so much to choose from," Bessie Jones says, "and so we learned to make the best of what we had." A deceptively simple statement from one who has lived more primitively than most of us can imagine. From the mingling of all these voices comes my title, *We Didn't Have Much, But We Sure Had Plenty.*

Doing the interviews was not easy. One of the greatest difficulties I met was asking people to speak of things about which they've learned to feel ashamed, or which don't fit the current social image of how things should be. Lack of money was one of the most difficult things for many people to talk about. I had to learn to communicate that my exclamations were of admiration, not of shock. There was one woman in the Ozarks whose interview changed dramatically after I casually mentioned that I'd lived with an outhouse for years, and she then "confessed" that she had gotten her first toilet when she was eighty years old.

Often, when women described the farm work they had done, they would say they "helped." When pressed for details, it would become clear that they regularly managed the dairy herd and the poultry, raised all the family's fruits and vegetables, and participated fully in planting and harvesting the field crops. To call all this work "helping" serves the useful social function of keeping male pride intact.

Another phrase that I heard so often that I began to wait for it to appear was some variation of "I'm a mannish woman," "I was my daddy's boy," "My mother said I should have been a boy." This often came hard on the heels of a defensive statement that she really did *not* like housework, and always preferred to be outside, said with a piercing stare. I would acknowledge that I didn't like housework either, and then often we would both laugh at some obscure joke on all of us. But I will never forget the first time I fully recognized the force of the statements about being like a man. It was early in the trip and I was in Kansas, interviewing a white-haired seventy-eight-year-old woman in a flower-sprigged dress and a knickknack-filled house. It had been a difficult interview to that point, and I kept wondering what I was asking wrong or what wasn't being said. Then she looked up at me and tears started sliding down her cheeks. "I should have been a man," she said. "I should have been a man. When we got the bigger farm, my husband wanted me to stay in the house. But I couldn't, I *belonged* outside!"

From her passion, and from all the other women who shared theirs with me, it came to me again that the horrible thing about silence is that eventually it takes from us our belief in our own reality. A whole culture has told us forever that rural women are "farmers' wives," not farmers. Yet every woman I met and spoke with had been in some way "a farmer," had done a vast array of jobs, had a multitude of skills. And lacking a language, a belief system, a vision of being simply human, they described themselves as "mannish" and "unwomanly." In a world where they had tremendous freedom to be themselves, they still lacked words for simply being themselves.

Another sharp realization that I had on this trip was that events that seemed to me dimly historical were very much alive to many people. I spoke with women who were told about slavery by slaves, a woman whose father fought in the Civil War, many women for whom the Dust Bowl and the Great Depression were personal experiences, another woman who traveled on horseback to New Mexico and homesteaded wild, unclaimed land. Myra Grant, who is only ten years older than I, tells in this book about walking a mile to return a penny's overpayment, something that was unheard of in my sophisticated urban neighborhood. It came to me over and over again how deprived I had been, despite sixteen years of excellent schooling, deprived as we all are when we are without history, when we aren't rooted in an understanding of ordinary people like ourselves.

It was impossible to guess when I started out which interviews would go well and which wouldn't. Sometimes women whose lives sounded wonderful turned out to be uncomfortable with introspection; they were doers, not talkers. Sometimes it seemed impossible to sum up so much experience in a few hours or a few conversations. "The crops burned up year after year, and I don't know what we found to eat," a woman said about the Depression. That one spare statement brought me a round of depression as I wondered if a novel wasn't a more truthful way to treat this material.

But there were also wonderful surprises along the way, new friends made, some connections that seemed to spring up immediately, other people I very nearly missed for one reason or another who touched me deeply. "I don't know why you want to talk to me," nearly everyone said. "I have nothing to say." And some of those women would still be speaking five hours later.

Choosing who would go into this book out of so many was very difficult. It is a process with which I will never be completely satisfied. After the first months on the road and fifty-six preliminary interviews, I spent a month in my sister's house in Atlanta listening to the tapes, trying to find a shape for the book, trying to decide whom I should visit on the return trip, with Judith Brown along to take photographs. For months I had been pondering how to translate rambling spoken conversations onto the printed page. The first tape I transcribed, with Irene Nixon's thick south Georgia dialect, made the problems even clearer.

Then came a crucial turning point. I was reading Robert and Jane Coles' *Women of Crisis* one night in Atlanta. I put the book down and realized that all the time I had been reading about a black itinerant farm worker, my mind's eye had been seeing a white, educated woman. Because, although the *words* in the book were the woman's words, the *language* was not her language.

It is very difficult to explain this distinction to anyone who has not struggled with transcription. But I became determined that I wanted to effectively translate the spoken voice onto the written page. In trying to do so, I discovered how *easy* it is to transcribe into standard

English, and how hard it was to make myself spell the words as they sounded or punctuate to re-create the rhythm of the speech. Sometimes I would have to play a statement over three or four times until I could finally visualize its form as a sentence. Tones of voice, except for emphasis, were very difficult to translate, for without the inflection or the humor in the voice, the sentence itself can take an entirely other meaning. Laughter, which rippled constantly through so many conversations, presented a difficulty I never did thoroughly solve.

If I had any doubt of the difficulty of this task, it was confirmed when, pressed for time, I sent several of the tapes to an experienced transcriber. What I got back was useless. Although every word was technically correct, there was no *life* there, the voice was missing. In reading those transcripts, once again I began to believe my eyes, to think the women themselves must have been dull.

Transcribing the tapes was, however, only the first step of the process. I had then to take the "voice" I was coming to be familiar with, and find some way to cut, edit, rearrange the material into a cohesive piece, as moving as the woman's original conversation. All I can say is that I hope these women themselves will be pleased.

The women in this book speak both with great uniqueness and with commonality. The differences I found in climate, culture, language, experience, were in some ways so vast as to be stunning. Jennie Cirone and Irene Nixon, for instance, must have sometimes thought me dim-witted when I couldn't understand a word they said. Myra Grant let me know that the world divided into two kinds of people: Mainers and everyone else. Each woman in the book brought her own blend of background, region, personal temperament, and experience to our conversations. But there is also a commonality to the book that needs explaining, for I have edited each individual piece knowing that it sits side by side with the others. If one woman speaks of a deeply fruitful marriage, if another speaks of a painful and badly troubled marriage, if one speaks of religion and spirituality, it does not mean that others have not shared any of these, and many more, experiences. It only means that the book is also intended to be read as a whole, to be a patchwork quilt of a period of time and a way of life.

There are silences too in this book, many stories that have yet to be told. There were things that were only spoken of when the tape recorder was off: anger at a family's dependency, a husband hospitalized for suicidal depression, a child bitterly separated from parents. There are the silences of those things that you never tell other people, and perhaps that you don't even tell yourself. There is the natural editing that is memory. "I only remember the good times," one woman told me, and she literally could not remember fifteen years of her long life. And there are the silences of those things taken so for granted they seem unnecessary to say.

So often listening to these women speak of the work they had done, I remembered the years I had struggled to dare to believe that I could build a barn, give shots to sheep, repair a pump; and I envied them their unconscious freedom. Then one night a woman said to me, "You know, it's difficult not to envy my daughters terribly. They have so many choices I never had."

"I will regret all my life that I didn't really talk to my mother," another woman said. "I never *really* asked her how she felt about her life, what her marriage was like, how she'd felt raising all of us. And my children come home now and I listen and listen about them, but nobody asks me what I think and feel." We were sitting up late at night in a farmhouse kitchen, talking with the cozy intimacy women so often share at odd moments. And I realized that I, who had traveled the country trying to understand the meaning of dozens of older women's lives, had never asked my own mother and grandmother the same searching questions. Had, in fact, let an age-old conspiracy of silence divide us, had continued with the arrogance of a younger generation to think that the women of my own family had nothing to teach.

It remains perhaps only to say that the women in this book are very ordinary people. They become special in the way that every person becomes special when they speak honestly, from the heart. "There's nothing important about me," they all said. But there is something very important about what they say. Truth-telling enriches our sense of the possible, and the stories of our lives in some way become our lives.

I set out a year ago, looking for the women who have come before, and I have been very richly rewarded. If my own life will in many ways be vastly different from theirs, I still have their endurance, their forbearance, their compassion, and their vitality to guide me. These are truly women who by our present standards did not have "much," and who by other standards have a plentiful lot to teach. They were our great-grandmothers; they are our mothers and grandmothers. They live with us, next door to us, down the road from us. For their honesty, I have profound admiration and gratitude.

Sherry Thomas

January 1980

I

PAST AS PRESENT

A Thankful Little
Irene Nixon

Irene Nixon is believed to be in her nineties, and lives in Lee County, Georgia. She and Lottie Jackson (who appears later in this book) have worked as field hands on the same farm since the early 1940s. Irene is a tiny woman who hauls her own firewood, raises her own vegetables, and maintains her own house. At the time of this interview, the farm on which she and Lottie had worked for over thirty years had just been sold to an agribusiness corporation and the two women were forced to move. Irene is a visionary who has endured more than most of us can imagine and still triumphs. There are few abstractions in Irene's life: time is measured by events, not years: children born, grown, and dead, crops harvested, storms that came and passed. In her life the supernatural is an immediate and personal experience.

My mama an them ain't *never* told us how old us was. When I'd go to 'em an say, "Mama how old I is?" she say, "Get away from here, madam, you're old enough to be no good!"

They ain't NEVER tell us our ages! But *now,* if a chile ain't but one year old, he can tell, if he two he can tell, on up. But us have never knowed!

I do know I was borned up in Sumter County, Georgia. I was born right up there where my husband died. My daddy was a share-cropper. I don' know how many chillun my mama had. There's so many, I couldn't tell you. Um huh. They's scattered ever which way. Um hum. Well now, I kin tell how many if I call out them names. They's muh sista Willy Lou, she's dead. An Lucille, me, Julia. An Anna, Clady, Sista, Dessa Mae, Lily Mae, an mmmm . . . I cain't call 'em there's so many of 'em . . . an Luster, an Two-Brother. That's eleven chillun an I'm the second one. The sista what died in Tampa that's the first an I'm next to her. An you know'd with all of 'em grown, you *know* I'm some old!

All'm but two was girls. I thinked the girls'd be the best. Yes, ma'am! A girl ain't hard to keep up wid. A boy, he'd run away, a boy, he'd be gone. A new dress to put on, that's about the worst trouble a girl is. Boys, they go off and get in devilment, not like a girl. Yeah'm boys is *tough* and mean. Cain't raise 'em, not like the Bible speak of it.

When I was a girl, I'd work from Monday mornin to Saturday night. Workin in our fields. We had corn, an cotton, an peanuts. It was hard times, yes ma'am! It was a time of trouble for me. I worked many times, *many* days an didn't eat a mouthful. I had a *mean* old daddy. I know he wus mean, cause he'd whup us to death. If folks was come to the house, you couldn't go an get a drink of water. No'm not if grown people was in there, you couldn't go in there. An I've laid down under the porch an then when my mother'd come, I'd be sleepin, an she'd carry me into the house. I'd be sleepin under the house. You see, Dad wouldn't let me come in the house. He was an old *bad* man.

When my mother an them be gone to town, to a show or somptin, I'd—I'd stay out doors *all* the time, where if he'd get at me, I could run. And he'd come out there makin wood, an he'd say, "You didn't come in the house when Lily was gone, you better not come in there now." Muh mother was named Lily Darver. Us called her Lil, us ain't never called her "Mama." Called our father Will. He was mean.

My mother was just as good a person as ever put her feet on the ground, my mama was good! My mama brought me buckets of somptin all the time when I was over there hidin, brought me somptin to eat. My dad wouldn't let me eat there. You see, now I hate to tell you bout him, but youse is a grown young woman—you see, he was an old BAD man. He'd be at us girls, you know . . . get in us . . . An us that wouldn't *do,* you know, us that'd say we'd call our mother, us that wouldn't do *nothin* like that, well he called it punishin. He'd let muh other sisters go a-frolickin an things, an I'd stay home all the time, didn't go nowhere. He called it self-punishin. That was his punishment, to bring me around to his way. But I hold out to the end. That was my daddy.

I had a *hard* time, that's the truth of it. Come up so hard. I'd be standin in the field by myself, an the cotton was high, cotton'd be higher than I be. An when I'd hear the wagon goin, I'd lay down there in the high cotton, keep 'em from seein me out there by myself all the time. I didn' want 'em to see me.

I've lived through hard times. An my mama'd cook a pie an go to the fields, an he'd let them eat out'n it, but wouldn't let me eat none.

See, that be *punishin* me. He'd get at all the girls thata way. All them that wud *do*. But I wouldn't do that myself. No! I'd wudda *died*. Cause I didn't have sense enough bout runnin away or nothin like chilluns got now. But I told the boss man, yes'm I told him. I telled him, God knows I did! I don' know how old I was when I got away. My mama wouldn't tell me how old I was. But muh brothers and sisters was little. Real little.

An the way I got away, the boss man know a white man that said somptin about goin away . . . he took me soon one mornin, when my daddy an them were off workin, when I could get off. If it hadn't've been fer him, I couldn't have got off, cause if I'd've stayed round there in the country in the wintertime, my daddy, he'd've killed me.

I went to Americus. An I didn't know no one. I got there, an I didn' know nothin bout goin nowhere by myself, you know. An the man carried me a piece in his wagon, an then I jest walked on by muh own self. When I got to Americus, the law carried me down to a house, a lady house that wud let me stay there. I was workin at the court-house, you know, I was washin towels, you know to live off, carryin them towels to the courthouse. An my daddy come up dere after me wif his shotgun! It was loaded. I had got my basket of towels an was carryin 'em to the courthouse, fore I could git there, he grabbed me. Course there was so many that was out, that see'd me, and they caught him. They put him in jail. That how I got away. An when he went to the chain gang an had made up his time, muh mama wouldn't take him back no more.

In Americus, I did what white folks wants. Worked in the houses, differnt ones and anothers. I'd get a little somptin, not much. Yeah'm we talkin about a *little* money. An when I got it, I thought I had bout a hundred dollars! They wasn't payin me anythin a day, jest givin me a somptin now an then. An I was jest as glad of it as if I had twenty dollars. Just gave me a little somptin. Not much. Sometimes nothin but somptin to eat. Somptin to eat. Mmmmm. I stayed in the house where I was workin. Weren't no workin folks then, they didn't *hire* no folks to work like they do now. You jest did the best you can.

Cause I'd say, "A little bit is better than none at all."

An I'd say that today. M'hmmmm. Have a thankful little to be blessed for yet. MMMMMM. I come up some hard. Sometimes, I be here by myself thinkin bout how I come up, an I be just quiet.

Yeah, I come up some TOUGH!

I only had one husband, the husband what died. I wadn't nothin but a *chile* when he got me. My chilluns was just little bitty little chilluns when he died. They was little bitty when I went to work down at Mr. Wade's, after muh husband died.

Muh husband could sew as good as any woman. If he'd get me to go anywhere for him, like to town or anyplace like that, I would put that cloth on the bed, an the scissors, an he would be done a-made somptin on the machine when I got back, an have it folded up on the bed! Yeah'm he could sew! An he'd cook, yeah'm he'd cook. I had a *good* husband, ceptin he was sure mean. He sure would whup me nights.

I'd say, "You won't!"

An he say, "I sure will!" cause he would tie me up! I would bring it on myself. I'd go off to frolics, go dancin an drinkin whiskey. An settin wif dis fella, an dat one. Didn' do nothin *bad,* you know, jes dancin. An some fella'd bring me on home. An then muh husband wud beat me. He tie me up to the tree. I knowed he was gonna do it, but I jest *had* to go. Couldn't stop myself from goin to frolics.

When you're wrong, you're due to pay up. Anybody know when they're right an when they're wrong. I jes wanted to go to frolics an I did. I jes had to *go*. I didn' have sense like girls have got now, when I was young. GOD KNOWS I didn't! That's the truth! If I had, I wouldn't have took the things I have took. I jes didn' have the sense. I should've runned away or somptin but I didn' know nothin bout things like that. Little chilluns now, they say, "You whup me an I'll run away." Oh, I runned away when I was jest a girl, but that were the white man that got me off.

I has three chillun. Two boys an a girl. My girl, Monk, just died here, I think she'll be dead six or seven years in August. I know one of muh boys is still livin. But I don' know where L.W. is at, couldn't find him when Monk died. I was fat clear to the birth of my girl, then I been little ever since. I had fits so bad, they said. Had fits *so* bad. I didn't even know she was in the world till the next day. I had convulsions. You know those houses got windows but weren't no window glass or nothin in them windows. You had to put quilts over the windows when it rained, an it were *dark* in there that day. I ain't knowed muh baby was in the world till I hear my sista—the one I told you died in Tampa—say, "Irene, you want to see your baby?"

"Baby," I says, "I ain't got no baby."

She says, "You got a little girl, you want to see her?"

An when she said that, I was *so glad*. So glad! So I hears the wind a-blowin, an she comes back with somptin wropped up.

An she says, "You want the baby in the bed with you?"

She put the baby in the bed and it's a wonder I ain't smothered the baby to death. I hugged her up so tight, it a wonder I ain't smothered her! I didn't know I had her. An when I woked up I feel muh stomach an I said, "Muh stomach's gone, but I sure ain't had no baby." No'm, I didn't feel a pain, nothin, if I had 'em, I didn' know it. Dr. Kelly said if it'd been one more hour afore he got there, I'd a been dead. He said my blood went to my head.

But I knowed when L.W. and Buddy was born. I nursed 'em with my breast, nursed Anna's with my breast too, muh sista's. I nursed them too, with mine. Cause muh sista had blue milk, she couldn't nurse them. We didn't use no bottles then.

Yeah'm I were workin in the field, hoein cotton an peanuts, an things, when mine was born. The day Buddy was born, my baby boy, I couldn't work. He had—he done turned round. An I came in from work, an honey I got me a lookin glass like that one yonder, an I laid it down on the floor, an I got over it an I look down. An honey, I could see his knotty head! I was lookin to see what was the matter wid me. I had to walk wide-legged, an I tried to set down on the step, but I couldn't set down. I looked in the glass, an I see'd his head! He was turned around. They carried me to Dr. Stadum—he was a good doctor —an he rubbed and rubbed an tried to rub him to turn him around, an he couldn't. He said I'd have to stay that way till time, said it wouldn't be long. Well, I felt like I was *blowed up* down there. I was havin pains, yeah'm, I was havin 'em! Had 'em clean till he was born. Dr. Stadum said it wouldn't be long. Just like he said, it wasn't long. I went to the doctor that day, an I had that baby the night of the next day. An I was havin pains bad. With his head down there like that. I had pains bad, m'hmmmm. An that's a miserable feelin, I'm tellin you the truth! Yes ma'am! I stayed in the house with my brother and his wife. Well, I'd be there by myself cause they was all workin, but when I was sick like that, my ma would come an see bout me bout every minute—you know, when she could get a chance to get away. She was Mr. Wade's cook.

An when L.W. was born, it was all right, but it just hurted me so bad. I jumped up, an the ceilin was so low, I jumped up an it just knocked me back down! I worked in the fields till I started havin my pains.

I had a husband when my chilluns was born, but when he died they was just little, couldn't even talk good. They's little bitty chillun when my husband died. An muh husband he talked to me as good as I'm talkin right now, that mornin. He got up an he done put on his Sunday clothes, dressed up. I didn't know who that was settin there, dressed up! Put on his shoes, his Sunday clothes, his Sunday hat, an ev-erthing. It scared us!

I said, "How come you put on your clothes?"

He said, "I'm a goin off."

I said, "Goin what?"

He said, "I'm goin off."

An then he was dead, just that quick. I knowed he was dead, cause I was down on my knees holdin his head, an the weight jes a keep a comin. He was fifty-four.

He said he'd seen his death the week before. He said it had a great big body, an great big eyes. He see'd it in the barn, an all the horses an mules came out whistlin an goin on, an he said he'd see'd it. An that was Jimmy's death, comin to him. You can see it, yeah you can! As far as that, you can see yours. Yeah, you can see your death! You may not know what you're seein, but you kin see it.

All of 'em dead now. All of muh schoolmates, an all of them white folks that I stayed on their place, an muh husband, an muh girl, all of them dead. M'hmmmmm. Got me here yet.

After death ain't all. After death, you got to go before the Judge, an you got to stan' right there. I wouldn't mind dyin, if dyin was all. But it ain't all, nmm, mmm.

I don' know how long I've been on dis farm with Mr. John. Ever since my husband been dead an that been . . . yeah, you know that he been dead and my chillun's got grown and got chillun, got grown chillun their own selves. Yes'm I got two great-grands. I come here after muh husband died, an he died when my chillun were little bitty little chilluns . . . Yeah'm . . . I've done *been* here!

I pulled peanuts, an pulled weeds, picked cotton, things like that. I ain't never cooked no breakfast. I'd ruther jes go on to the field. I hates to cook so bad. Yeah'm I be hungry but I'd make it. If I could jes get me some snuff, I'd make it. I kin be *sooo* hungry right now an put a little bit of snuff in my mouth, an it'll go right away. I'd ruther work in the fields, ruther cut yards, ruther do *anything* than cook. Now two things I hate, that's cookin an ironin. That the truth! My sista cooked fer me sometime, an Lottie cooked fer me sometime.

At da other places, us went to da fields at sunrise, but us didn' go like that at Mr. John's. Us went later an jes worked till twelve o'clock. He was good to us, the best one I ever worked with, from a girl on up to this age. Wid Mr. John, we stay out for lunch till he come back. Lord! At dem other places, we be out in da field at sunup an it be sundown when us come home. You stop an eat but you stay right dere in da field. I ain't struck nair a good un till I come down here. Us didn't work till no sundown for Mr. John!

I been to places where you pulled fodder, took up fodder by the lantern light. Be so wet sometimes, *Lord!* I don' know what to say, be like the *chain gang* then! I ain't ever seen slavery times, but I believe it was *worse* in slavery times. Slavery times, that *was* a tough time. Cause they wud sell your chillun jes like they sell cows an hogs an things. The boss man would.

But I couldn't a worked no harder. I worked *hard!* You wasn't makin much money in those days, jes a little bit of somptin. Sometime five dollar a week. That were the high. I worked so hard, till I come to Mr. John. I worked *so* hard, couldn't do no harder work on a chain gang.

I could pick cotton, and that's the truth! I could pick a bale of cotton in two days. Some days, I'd pick a bale of cotton in one day, sure as you're born. I used to pick two and three hundred pound ever day. An pick cotton in Thelma's sack too, fer Thelma to go home cook me my dinner and bring me somptin to the field. Her cooked fer her an me both! I used to could work, now that's the truth!

Thelma, she had a husband out there pickin too, but she picked-ed by herself and he picked-ed by himself. They didn't put their cotton together. An I'd pick fer her when she cooked. Yeah, I used to work! As the song say, "I'm a good old wagon, but honey I done broke down!"

An that don' say nothin bout the peanuts I stacked up, I put up. Ooooh, I used to could put up peanuts! Wasn't nair a person could put 'em up so quick as I.

Down at Mr. J.B.'s one time, I beat the field, beat the whole field pickin cotton. Beat all the whole field and there were a heap of 'em! I went to visit my brother, an I said wud Mr. J.B. care if I went out there an worked a little bit? An my brother say that he see Mr. J.B. an he tell him. An that day, Mr. J.B. say he give fifteen dollar to the one what could pick the most cotton. I beat the field, I picked four hundred an somptin pounds, there was some cotton out there! That the truth! Mens and women workin out there. But they got mad with me, they ain't never wanted me to come back there agin. Mr. J.B., he gave me that fifteen dollar.

I have done *did* on this farm. I was doin field work, an den I stopped down at the field. You see, I was old enufft to go . . . after that, I worked up at Mr. John's house. I worked up there bout fifteen year. I had a regular job up there when those chilluns was little. I had to clean up, you know, an iron, iron twice a week, hang out da clothes dat Miz Martha would wash, take care of the flowers, all them things to do. And Dave and Ed they was little bitty little chillun. I've bathed 'em many times an put 'em to bed an stayed up wif 'em many times when Mr. John and Miz Martha'd be comin in at night. Sometimes, Mr. John'd catch me sleepin, I'd be so sleepy. Miz Martha sure was nice to me, and Mr. John was. I had to stop. I wudda fell dead at the ironin board, you know, my arms had give out with the arthritis. My arms jes give out. Yeah'm I work for her clean till she fix her brick house down there in Appleton an she moved-ed dere, an then I quit. After I went to gettin my little money [Social Security], you know, I stopped workin then. I was well old when I start to gettin my money.

I had put my garden in out here till I heard I had to move. Then, I took it down, so's I kin move the chicken wire. Reckon wherever I go, I'll put in a garden, whenever I have the time to fix it. When I was workin in the fields I'd work the garden on Saturdays. Mr. John didn't hold with his hands workin on Saturdays. He's a good man, an I hope the Lord blesses him. Course, he's fractious, he *is* fractious. It jes his way. It ain't from the heart, what he sayin ain't from the heart. He jes *on* this minute an *off* the next. But it didn' worry me cause it were jes his way, an I knew his heart were good.

Everbody jes got a way, jes got their *own* way, that's the truth! I don' know what my way is like, but I don't like that way of on today and off tomorrow. I don' like that kind. I like the "keep on" kind, jus keep right on. I always did jes what I wanted to do. If I want to do, I do. I jes *go* when I want to. I didn't have *sense,* though, when I was a chillun, that I got when I growed up. Oh, I been gettin mannish, I reckon. Yes sir, gettin mannish. I jes always wanted to go, to a frolic, or anywhere, an I always did jes go. I'd take any dare when I were younger. You know, got to be my *own* woman.

But I done come down now. I don' even like no rioty places, *nothin* like that now! I used to drink whiskey, but I don' drink a drop of it now, I cain't *stomach* it. But I still love snuff. I want it worser when I go to bed than ever, but I cain't keep it in my mouth now, ain't got enough teeth. Seem like I spit three time, an that snuff is gone!

I ruther be a woman than a man! Yes ma'am, ruther be a woman! They things is so sorry, there ain't no good in 'em. God's takin 'em, he's takin 'em all away. With the little company I have, I wouldn't want nair a one near to me, that's the truth. Those things don' want to work, an jes want somebody to work an take care of 'em, they kin get out of my house! They git out or I'd git out mighty quick! Course, I don' know bout all mens, but I know the biggest portion of 'em ain't no good. Jes want somebody to take care of 'em. The old men, they'll tell you quick, "I want somebody what got money." There was one that used to admire me, so that I be dead an he get my money. If he knowed where it was at, an if'n I had any! They jes ain't—they jes ain't fittin er *nothin,* I don' know what to say about 'em! Make me so *mad.*

They tell you straight out, "I want a woman what got money."

I said, "Well, if I had any, you sure wouldn't get it!"

I could've gotten married. I could marry right now if I want to. But marry, if I marry it'd jes be to have a company-keeper. But I wouldn't want nair a company-keeper talkin bout he want my money. I'd jest lead him right to the *door!*

Muh girl Monk, she used to came all the time. She came *all* the time, afore she died. She were company to me. She tole me the last time she was here, she asked me to let her sleep wid me. An I tole her, I couldn't sleep wif no one.

She said, "Mama, let me sleep wif you."

I said, "Monky"—I called her Monky, but her name were Christine—I say, "I don' want you to sleep wid me. I cain't rest in da bed wif someone." Well, I tried to settle, but I couldn't. An she said, "Oh, Mama, let me sleep wif you!" So she did.

That mornin, she said, "Mama, you know what? I been comin all these years to see you, but you know what? I rested better last night than since I ever been comin up here."

That what she said. An the next news I hear bout her, she was dead. Mr. John brought me the telegram. It were an accident what killed her.

Yeah, it just this way. A person may not believe it, but some folks is short-lifed and some folks is long-lifed. That jus the way it is. Jus like some trees live longer than all the others. It got to be somptin mighty good dat you do to live dat long life. OOOOOOH! It been hard! But the Lord let the bottom rail come to the top sometimes!

I don' know why, I jus say everthing done made a change. Cause it ain't religious times like it was when I was comin up. You know it ain't, cause folks would just come out of da fields, off of dem mules, slip on a dress, an go on to da church, *walk!* Now, if you cain't ride, you won't hardly go to the church. Heap of folks ain't got nothin but sin. Folks pulled so far apart now. An they don' like one another. But it just the Bible fulfillin. I know when I was a chile, I hear Mama an them talkin about things would be flyin in da air, like birds, great big things wud be flyin. But that was a *long* time ago, my mama's, an Granmama's, an Granpa's lifetime, an so dese airplanes what we see now, dey's it. It's the Bible fulfillin. You know some people got chillun and the chillun'll fight the parents? How come? Cause the Bible says, daughters'll be agin mothers, mothers'll be agin daughters, fathers'll be agin sons, sons'll . . . Well, us done lived to see it. That is the truth!

I seen times when it look like it gonna be a great big storm, my mama an dem say, "Sista, sista, you'd better come on! Look like it gonna be a mighty big storm. Well, if the Lord take us, he take us all together!" Well, that ain't no more! Folks don' stick together no more.

An look at Daniel! You couldn't get someone to go in dere wif a lion if'n you had a tractor, nowadays. Couldn't pull one in wif a tractor! But Daniel he had the faith, an he walked right in there. An the Lord locked the lion's jaw so he couldn't do nothin to Daniel. I cain't read much, but Uncle Shep used to read the Bible to us on a Sunday. Us would come down there, him was an *old* man. He was a good reader. An you know that God is a good god!

I'm scared of water, always have been. Course now, I knowed, I got sense enough to know this: that the thing you scared of ain't the danger. Now I'm scared, an I ain't gonna make out that I ain't scared, when I *know* what I am is scared. Like the Bible say, be just what you is.

And I said, that what I be is jes scared! But I got sense enough to know that when life gives out, you're goin *right there,* if it be on the highway, or in the woods, or at the fish farm, or anywhere. An I know that you don' know what's your time or where's your place till you come to it. Yet and still, I'm more scared of water than of anything else. Now, if I looked at it right, I wouldn't be. If I was to look at it right. Only thing is, you cain't hide what you be. You is what you is. And I know one thing, water an wind, an fire, is dangerous things. The old earth kin be mean to you.

Heap of folks think if they die, they jes die. But that ain't all. Like they say in the song, "There's a little more." I wouldn't mind dyin, if dyin was all, but it ain't.

God don' take back what he give a person. Just like he dunned wid me. I *know* I been borned agin. I KNOW IT! Since I been over here in this house. When I stayed over yonder at Mr. John's other farm—I know Mr. John made three crops while I was over there—I see'd the *same* thing I see'd in this house. I see'd it over here twice, an I think I see'd it over there twice. I don' know what it represents, but LORD I hope I be *caught* when the sun goes down, if I'm tellin a story. I done seen myself flyyyyyyyyin, flyin, *flyin!* I had one leg drawed up behind me, an my arms out flyin. I saw the folks down in the yard lookin up at me, sayin, "Irene, you said you could fly." Sayin "She sure is flyin!" And that the truth. An I'd fly *all* around, an come back an light right down on da doorstep, an come right on in the house. Jus to show you how pure God holds you, I got up the next morning an put my foot up dis way, an my arms out that way, an I couldn't fly a bit! But I have seen it so many times, an if that ain't the truth, I hope I get *caught* when night come!

An I'll tell you another thing. I know I done been born. Since I been in dis house. I started out one time, I was travelin, an I got to a big old black greasy place, it look like it should have been a turpentine still or somptin. An the man had done put gates up an he done told me, "Don' come through here no more." So I went the wrong way, an I went on. Then I stood up an I didn't know where in the world I was; I stood up an I said, "Lord, I am lost." I said, "I don' know where I'm at. *Please* let me see somebody where I could ask 'em if'n I'm on the right road."

I went on, an I went on, an I went on, an I see'd the water. An old man come behind me.

I said, "Mista, where is I'm at? I don't know where I'm at," I say, "I'm lost." I said, "I kin see the road across there, but all this water, I cain't cross it."

I could see the road jes came to the water, an then it stopped. The man had a stick, it was an old man, but a white man. An he had a stick, one of these walkin sticks like the Bible call a crook. An he hit that water, an that water parted aside, an I walked on across. Now that's the truth from my heart!

An when I was first startin, callin myself to pray to git religion, it was a train that come along, an it was jest as black as smut, as the way train smoke is. An the old train was singin, it was singin: [she sings] "Boong a loong a boong a loong a booong." So I was standin out dere wif two or three others, and dem done got on, an I couldn't get on. An the train was jes a pullin off, singing "Boong a loong, boong a looong."

So I said, "Lord, dem folks done left me, an what do I do? I don' know where I am at, an dey done gone an left me."

Somptin said, "Ireney, you jus stan' dere, you jus stan' dere."

After a while, I hear another train comin, an it was singin bout "I am climbin up Jacob's ladder." An it was jest as white as a sheet, that train was, jest as *white as a sheet.* It got to dere, an it stopped. An the folks see'd me standin out dere, jes my one by my *lone* self. An He come to me, an He squared me so. He squared me so, look like I could hear my gut bubblin in me, "Bubbalabababala"! I could hear him breathin so deep.

He said, "Your sins are forgiven an your soul is set free!"

He took my hand, an He led me up dere, an He started singin bout "I am climbin Jacob's ladder." An when I got on dat train, it started off an the train was singin, "every round go higher, higher!" An the train was goin straight up to the sky jes like that. Honey, I *seen* some good *dreams,* that's the truth! I seen the way in my dreams.

One night, when I stayed over yonder on Mr. John's other place, an it looked-ed like it was gonna storm, oooooh, the clouds looked-ed so *bad,* like a tornado. An it was there bout sundown, an I knowed I couldn't make it over to here afore night. Wif that bad cloud, that would've made it darker. An I had a big dresser jes like this. An I put it over by the door. An I said, "Lord, have mercy. I'm *scared* over here all by myself." An I sighed.

An somptin called me three times. Said, "Irene. Irene. Irene, blow da lamp out an go to bed. I kin keep back all the hurt on the land."

An I ain't been that scared of storms agin, from that day to this one. An that's the truth! I seen good dreams. God showed me *good* dreams! He don' take back what He give you. What He give you, you have. What you have, you have. He don' come *every* time you call, He knows jes *when* to come! He don' come at every call, but at the needed time, He'll be there! Jus the *needed* one. That how it been fer me, an I got a thankful little to be blessed fer, yet!

My Daddy's Boy
Maude Hunter Dyke

Maude Dyke lives in Ashton, West Virginia, along the Ohio River Valley. Her house sits on a hill above a mountain "holler," made fertile by repeated river floodings in her childhood—"before they built the locks," Maude says. Her father was a soldier in the Confederate Army during the Civil War, and that period of history is vividly present for her.

Maude was married and divorced twice, unusual for her generation. She was a nurse and midwife, operated a small sawmill, helped start the district's first secondary school, and farmed with her father.

At the time of this interview, Maude's daughter was sixty-nine years old, and Maude herself was eighty-eight. A few days after I was there, Maude suffered a crippling stroke.

I always was my daddy's boy. I always stayed with Daddy, outside. And of course, Mother was rather old, cause she was in her forties and Dad was in his fifties when I was born. I was a very late baby.

There's six years between my last sister and me. I just always follered my daddy, cause I reckon I just always loved to be outdoors, from a little baby on, once I could walk. I set between the horses' reins, on their necks, while Daddy'd be plowin. And I always worked with him— whatever Dad was doin, I was doin. We plowed, he grubbed tree shoots. I would plow the long rows, and Daddy would plow the short rows, on account of the turnin. I must have been around nine or ten, then.

I helped to build this house—oh, I thought I was the biggest one of the whole bunch and I wasn't but five years old. Daddy cut the trees down, and he'd hitch the chain around. Then I'd ride the horse and pull those logs down to the mill. And I wasn't but five years old! Oh, there was never anything too big that Daddy didn't think I could do. And I nearly always got by with it too! We sawed all this lumber for the house. Then the lumber that's smoothed—floors and ceilings, that sort of thing—we'd haul that to the mill and have it planed, and then we'd haul it back with the four-horse team. But we didn't consider those things too hard. Daddy could turn off more work than anyone you ever saw, he never got in a hurry, just worked the same speed, but when the day was done, he'd done more work than anybody else. And that's the way I work, too. I always worked with Daddy, whatever he did. Why, he even had me made a little mattock, and I went with him whenever he went out!

Our old house was three big rooms with a breezeway in between, it was a huge house. There wasn't any rooms as small as these: big square rooms, you know. And Grandfather hewed out the logs himself. And when they were put up, they were cut out in grooves so they fitted together. There was three big rooms upstairs and three downstairs.

There was no locks on the river at that time, and ever spring the back-water would get in two or three times. An Mother would have all that cleanin, she'd put everthing upstairs, but still. And we'd have to white-wash all the logs inside again. I kin remember the fireplaces, they was huge. The one in the kitchen had the cranes that they cooked by, and the hurths was great big stones, an they'd pull the live coals out, an cook there. They had the great big skillets and these lids to go on them. Then they'd put these live coals up over these lids, and that would cook the whole thing, you see. And whatever was cooked in those skil-lets was delicious!

Now we never did have money. Oh, jest barely enough to git by with. An pay our taxes. But we always had lots of food. That's the way people lived in those days. And Daddy always did that, because we worked the garden an the truck patches, *then* we'd go to the field. But the truck patches always came first, so we'd always have food. You never sold your vegetables, you'd *give* a neighbor anything, but you never sold nothin.

We always had lots of company. And Daddy always, stranger'd come along the road and talk to him, mealtime'd come, well "you come along to the house and get you. . . ." An that's the way he was. An we always called it "the house beside the road," and I still call it "the house beside the road." I usually feed everybody. Now this winter, I've not been so I could do very much cookin. Long 'bout the time I get a meal ready, well, the pain starts. And the doctor says I just cain't do it. I like to cook, I've always liked to cook. I've lived by myself an awful lot, and I always did cook myself three meals a day.

When I had this chest pain this winter, I'd talk. I mean, I'd just rattle, rattle, rattle. And wadn't nobody here, I'd talk to myself. And that's something I never did do. So I said to myself one day, "Why I'm a-talkin to myself! I've just got to stop that, that's old, old people's ideas."

I sew a lot and I crochet. I just cain't set an not do anything, an the doctor don't want me to do anything. But I told him that I had to cook for myself. And I had to make my own bed.

He said, "Why make your own bed?"

I said, "Cause I don't want no wrinkles in it!" When I was nursing, I was always very particular that I never let a wrinkle be under my patients' hips. Nurses are not that particular now.

I took up nursing when Virginia was eight years old. Virginia's my daughter and she's sixty-nine now. I wasn't an R.N., but I always nursed for the *best* doctors. And I always read up on everything. When I come back home to live with Daddy after my mother died, I—oh, I brought lots of babies into the world around here. Until we had to have the license. People depended on me to have their babies, instead of gettin the doctor to do it. An I never did have any trouble but one time, and the woman hemorrhaged. They was so poor they didn't have anything and I knew I had to do something *right now*. And I had read in the *Reader's Digest* just a week or two before that if anything ever happened that a mother was hemorrhaging when a baby was being born, to use vinegar. Well, I went in the kitchen and there set a new jug of vinegar, an I just grabbed it and I had some clean cloths in my nursing bag. And I just wet them and I went up in there, grabbed that uterus. And the doctor was on his way there, an I just held onto that uterus till he got there.

And he said, "Well, where did you ever hear of that?"

I said, "I read that in the *Reader's Digest,* last week."

And he said, "Well, you've saved her, that's all."

When it was time, people just would come for me. They didn't pay me, you know. And I had a horse, and I'd whistle for him in the night. Any other time, he was hard to catch, but in the night he'd come to me every time. And of course, all these things was great experiences, each baby was different, you know. Every mother that ever had a baby, each, all, is a different birth.

I'm a member of the Morris Chapel Church, now I *do* want you to put that in. I mean, since I was fifteen. And the Upland Farm Woman's Club; and the Daughters of the Confederacy, Chapter 150. And the Democratic Woman's Club at Point Pleasant. So I'd have to be a Southerner, you know.

One time at a meeting, a fella said to me, "Are you going to vote for him?"

And I said, "No!"

"Why?" he asked.

"Well, Ben," I said, "bein a Democrat is ninety-seven per cent of your chance of goin to heaven, and I'm not a-goin to change it!"

Virginia was born when I was a little past sixteen. She was born in February an I was sixteen in January. I shouldn't have got married so young, but I jest did. I think of my greatgrandchildren now, that older one is way older than his years. Maybe I was jest the same way.

I don't know how I learned mothering—just nature, I guess. An then, my mother was an invalid an she was here with me. What I didn't know, she did. When I first got married I kept on livin here. See, Mother was an invalid and I had to take care of her. Then when I did go to housekeeping, why we had several different girls stay with Mother. But my daddy kept on farmin as long as he lived. At eighty-five, he was still doin all the farmin on this place.

I had three other children, besides Virginia, 'ceptin they didn't live. Two of 'em died with the flu, the two little boys. But the little girl was stillborn. One of the boys was four years old and the other was nine days old when they died. This little boy, he was just a wonderful child.

This one old neighbor used to always say, "Maude, you're never goin to raise Howard, he's too good. That chile is jest too good an too nice to live."

An I said, "Well, if the Lord takes him, then he jest lent him to me for a little while." And he did take him, with the flu. People don't realize now what the flu was like, back in World War I.

All four of my children were born in my first marriage. I never had no children with my second husband cause I'd had my hysterectomy by then. I had those children almost as fast as I could have them. Then I had to have my uterus taken out. I had a tumor, an I hemorrhaged till I couldn't even raise my head up, before I ever give up to be operated on. That was at the time of the very first hysterectomies.

I liked married life, but my last husband, Russ, drank so. An we could never go anyplace in a car, cause I never knew when he'd be sober. An I never had no patience with him, anyhow. Cause I was never used to it. When I was real little, my sister married a fella that drank all the time. She'd get him to sit down an rock me, cause she knew that if he rocked me to sleep, he'd rock himself to sleep too! So I always had it in me that I would never live with a drunkard. An Russ got to drinking. He wasn't like that when we got married. He was a good person. Everybody loved him. People said to me, "Well, I don't see why you couldn't have lived with him."

"Well," I said, "I just didn't have to."

We didn't have no fallin out, but I never had to live with a drunkard. I didn't give as much thought to what other people would think as I give to my own self. Cause he spent everthing we had. Till I didn't have anything except this farm.

An I said, "Now, don't you ever sign anything against this farm. This is *my* farm! An you never had nothing to do with it. When it comes to you drivin your train, I never had nothin to do with runnin your engine; an you're not goin to do nothin with my farm!"

I had inherited this farm, and I didn't intend for him to get it. My brother and my father never drank, and my brother-in-law jest couldn't help himself. But he drank up everthing they had. He drunk up a big river-bottom farm they had. I don't mean a little farm, but a *big* farm! Prohibition didn't help much. I didn't vote for it. That was when us women first got the vote. I thought it was just foolish that we couldn't vote. I've worked in politics all my life. I was committee-woman down here, and I got all but three to vote Democratic. And I never did find out who those three were!

The last time I was out in the garden out here was last year. And I made it out to the road, down to the bottom of the hill, and I was settin there—I always take my chair, my lawn chair—and keep it along at the end of my row so I kin sit down in it. So I got out there an I couldn't get no farther, so I just set down. An I thought, first one that goes up the road, I'm gonna hail him down to help me get to the house. So it was Dan came along, an he said, "Granny, I'll take your things up to the house."

I said, "Honey, it's takin me up to the house that you've got to do!"

He said, "What's the matter with you?"

An I said, "I cain't make it." So I had to promise that I wouldn't go down to work in that garden no more. I'll go down this year an try to help with the plantin some, but I jest cain't raise a whole garden. The doctor says I just musn't do it. I've got this chest pain, an I've got so stooped. So stoop shouldered and all, where I was just as straight as could be. But I jest give over to this pain. An he says, it isn't a disease, it's just a warnin of a stroke or a heart attack. An I wouldn't want either one, cause my daughter last spring had a light stroke. In her right side, an her hand works all the time. When she first come in the house, I seen right then that somethin's wrong.

And she said, "Now, Mother, don't you sympathize with me! I cain't stand fer people to sympathize with me. Now, I cain't stand it!"

"Well," I said, "honey, Mother is goin to sympathize with you, regardless of what you say. *Mother* isn't people. People is people, but Mother is Mother."

She was never sick much in her life. But now, the doctors told her that she could have another one anytime. And she was jest combin her hair!

Everthing's changed, everbody's changed. I was happier when I was young. Now, our father never said one time that we *had* to do something. He'd say "Babe, don't you think it's time for us to better go to work?" "Don't you reckon that corn'll never be fixed if we don't get at it?" We plowed corn both ways, what there wouldn't be much weeds left. But we did everthing with the spirit that it was *fun*.

I think this country is just in a turmoil, a terrible turmoil. It cain't get much worse, less'n we have a civil war or somethin. The trouble is, there's too many strikes. Everbody's on strike. These factories all along the river here are all on strike. People don't want to work anymore. The Bible is bein fulfilled, but as the Bible says, "The time is not yet."

I could die anytime now. That's how I live, knowin that anytime . . . I've been in a dyin condition all winter now. But I've always been so active and I think you kin stay active when you're old, if you don't lose your willpower. Now, my sister lost her willpower and they had to put her in the nursing home. She was six years older than me and she died this spring, she was ninety-four. I'm the last one of our generation, the last one of my mother's side and the last one of my father's side. . . .

I've had three operations an that doctor said I could take pain more than any woman he ever saw. An I still can take pain. But this winter it makes me nervous, pain makes me nervous. The doctor says, it's mostly in my nerves.

He says, "Don't you never get mad?"

"No," I says, "I've learned me not to. Because, if I get mad, I get the worse end of it, cause it makes me sick afterwards."

And so, if I see anything that provokes me, or crosses me, I just leave it. I wasn't always like that, no. Now, it always took a good bit to *make* me mad, but when I got mad, I was mad all over! But I just don't do that anymore.

If you'll stay, in forty-five minutes now, I'll have some hot bread from the oven. Mother always used to make salt-risin bread. An Daddy always loved the heel. We'd be down to the field, an Daddy'd say, "Babe, don't you think you should run down to the house, get us a can of buttermilk? And maybe your mother'll have the bread done!"

II

FAMILIES

Making the Best
Bessie Jones

Bessie Jones is sixty-six years old and a great-grandmother, living in Capitan, New Mexico. In 1932, she and her family homesteaded a ranch in semidesert country, where she lived for forty-two years with her husband. Their way of life for much of that time was very like the way pioneer settlers lived in the 1800s.

In 1975, Bessie's husband died suddenly of a heart attack. A year later, needing a cataract operation, Bessie finally gave up ranching and moved permanently into town. Our talk took place out on the ranch where she spent most of her life. Two of Bessie's granddaughters came along to see what this was all about.

At first when I left, I missed this place real bad, because my husband and I had lived in this house for, oh, about twenty-five years. And Milt and I built it all up from scratch. We did have a good marriage. We were just a *union*, you know. And 'course, we lived out here. And ranch people where you don't have a lot a neighbors, I think have a better union, cause we *have* to. We have each other. Milt helped me in the house and I helped him outside. And we *loved* each other. Maybe that's the old-timey love, the old-fashioned love.

But now I *wouldn't* want to come back here without him. No. Oh, if somthin happened that one of my kids had to come back or somthin, I could come back. But I'm beginning to get satisfied with town too. But it was quite a change. We were married, my husband and I, for about forty-two years and we lived them all right here; be back and forth when we had to go off sometimes to make some money to-ah-make a *livin,* but we always came back. This was *home.*

We stayed in love with each other all those years. Well, it seems like it's a rare thing nowadays. But when we were young and married, we married for life. We didn't do like the younger generation now. And our mothers taught us, "When you are old enough to get married, you get married for life. Not just here today and gone tomorrow." So I think we were brought up with that and we just naturally felt that way. We found, or we thought that we'd found, the right person. Milt and I were lucky that we both loved each other. And he was a good man. I wasn't as good a woman as he was a man, but then there wasn't any use him knowing that! Well . . . he was a good, kind, gentle, patient man. And I was brought up from a high-strung family, a kinda high-strung person. But we were both lucky to have each other, when I see other people. Cause Milt didn't drink and stay away from me for long times, you know, like a lot of other people did. A lot of men drink, go off like this and leave the woman at home where she *cain't* go anywhere. *See,* we only had one car, and if he left, he left in the car. And I was left *alone* out here with the kids. And it's a long ways to the next neighbor, you know, eleven miles. The only thing that ever really worried me about it was I was 'fraid the kids might fall down the cistern and what *would* I do? An I thought, well, some way the Lord'll give me a ladder to put down there an I'll crawl down there, pick 'em up, an we'll crawl on out!

I have quite a few widowfriends up here and some of 'em been married for a second time. Well, I guess I was jest set in my ways with this one man with forty years of life, so I'm afraid I'm set in ways that wouldn't be up to a new husband! I never thought I'd be a widow. Oh, no, I was going to die first! I made a mistake!

Oh, if I had Milt back today, why I'd fuss at him, sure I would. That's natural. That's life. You won't change your life like that. I'd fuss about little things. Well, you know, sometimes he'd go to sleep on that couch when I didn't think he ought to be goin to sleep. We oughta get out and cut the weeds out *there,* somthin like that! It had to be "we," we worked together.

We weren't unusual for our generation. I think we all did it. I was just lucky that Milt didn't drink and carouse around. On ranch life, I think it takes both of us, for *everthing.* For the people that were out here, these homesteaders, I'd say *most* of us had to work together, men and women, to make a go of it. Cause, remember, this was in time of Depression, see.

My daddy was a trader, and that meant buyin this house one day and sellin it another. My mother went in, fixed it up real nice and he'd trade it off for a piece a land. But it was his desire in life sometime to have a homestead. And then when they came out here, livin in this dugout, it wasn't what he thought it was gonna be. So they went back to Texas, and Milt and I decided to stay on out here. We weren't married when we all came up here, but we were when Mother and Daddy decided to leave.

We each homesteaded a section [640 acres]. That is, my daddy did, and my sister and brother-in-law did, and Milt (which was my husband later on) did. Three sections in all. Then later my cousin filed on another section, so in all, there's four sections to this ranch now. You see, it's *raw* land that you file on, there was *nothin* here. You had to build a house to live in, and you had to put other improvements on it, fencin and barns. And you had to live on it seven months a year for three years, then you'd apply for it.

I was nineteen years old when my daddy came up here in thirty-two. See, I couldn't file because a woman had to be twenty-one, so I didn't file on a section myself. My mother, my daddy, and my widow sister and her little girl, and my other sister, Jewell, and her husband, and Milt Jones, and I all came out here. See, we all came together. My daddy told Milt that he would help him prove up if Milt would help drive the cattle up from Texas. They did it in a wagon and it took thirty days to drive those cows. But eventually, after we had proved up all the pieces, all the rest of 'em left. Jest Milt and I stayed.

When we first came, the house we built was a dugout, you know, dug down into the ground with just the roof and a little bit of wall aboveground. There wasn't much lumber out there then. There was two rooms to that dugout and there was a little attic up above with just a ladder that would be let down. My sister and her little girl slept up there. And then—why, you know, Milt slept in the barn! That's where he was most of the time, anyway! Then, when he got his little shanty built, he'd stay up there. And then he'd come down here, and we'd all work together.

We dug cisterns to catch the rain, and used cistern water in the house. But we would haul the drinking water from the neighbors' well. And, course, we had the outside uh . . . we didn't have a—I mean, we had an outhouse. So we didn't need so much water. Milt dug a cistern there at my dad's place and it was about twenty foot deep and six or eight foot straight across it. And that would last quite a long time. Just for washin water. And see, we washed dishes in a dishpan, we didn't wash dishes in a sink. You didn't have to use much water washin dishes in a dishpan! We had wood stoves in that dugout, we had a cookstove and we also had a heater. And we had to go twenty miles, must have been at least twenty miles, up into the mountains to get wood. I believe we lived fifteen years down in that dugout.

Milt and I married in January of nineteen thirty-four. And we'd been married a year or so, when Daddy and Mother went to Texas. Milt and I were together *all* the time. Whatever one did, the other one did. If he wanted me to help him, I'd say, "Well, dry the dishes for me." Well, that's the way we *courted,* really. When we moved out here with my mother and daddy, we were all together an the only way at all that Milt an I could talk to each other was that I would do the dishes ever night and he would dry them. Well, they *would* leave us together in the kitchen!

We lived in the dugout and we had the one light bulb from our own generator. Sometimes it worked, and sometimes it didn't! See, it was run by the wind, and if the wind didn't blow, you couldn't have any power. We had the old kerosene lamps, and we had a little old

Aladdin lamp and it gave *real* good light! And down there, as I say, we just had to get water out of the cistern. I had a pot, a big old black pot, and you'd draw up water and put it in the pot and heat the water, and then you'd wash your clothes, and then you had to boil 'em, an rub 'em again! But Milt always helped do the washin too. Until we had our first youngster, and then he said he believed we needed a washin machine, it was too much washin to do! So we bought a washin machine. Then, I would heat the water in the pot, put it in the washin machine—it was a gas washer—and start the motor. Much easier!

And then we were living in the dugout when we first got a gas refrigerator. Oh my! Did we think we had *really* gone to town then! An the way it was made, it had a little compartment in the middle that had four little ice trays. So I put the ice in a jar and filled up those four little trays, cause it took nearly all day to make ice. But that way we could have ICE TEA.

We built this house in nineteen fifty-two, and we lived in it ten years before we got electricity. The Rural Electric came through in nineteen sixty-two. My kids were grown 'fore we got the electric. Reason we didn't get it till so late was we was in a kind of out-of-the-way place. We were eleven miles from the nearest ranch, so they couldn't just drive up and put a pole in our yard!

It's hard for my daughter to remember how we lived. She'll say, "Mother, I don't remember that."

She'd say, "When we were young we didn't have a lot of things other people had, but I don't remember it."

And I said, "Well, we didn't have as much as some people, but we made the best of what we had. And when you do that, it doesn't make any difference if you have a lot or if you have a little."

And if you've never had it any different, well you think it's all right. But everbody else was havin it hard too, Jaunita and them were havin a hard time just gettin through life, just like we were. All of us was. Maybe other people had a little more than some. We didn't measure that by anything.

We went into debt to get some sheep. We had to herd these sheep and bring 'em in ever night, cause we didn't have any fences. Milt dug cisterns out in the pastures, and we'd pull water up in a bucket to water them sheep. I believe we bought a hunderd and fifty at first. The Roswell Production Company lent us the money to do this. And then the next year we went ahead an paid off what we owed 'em, so they let us borry the money to fence. So we fenced our land, and then years later, we drilled a well. Six per cent was pretty high interest back then. We didn't make any money off those sheep for a good many years, cause we put it all back into the land, see. We had just a piece of raw material there. And we did all the work ourselves. We farmed a little piece of land too. We raised corn one year, and then we raised cane. Then it seemed like there wasn't enough water, so we quit. I don't reckon we had but forty acres we farmed. Might not seem like much, but we didn't have any mechanical equipment at all. And see, we didn't have any way of makin a livin. Course, it was the same way with everbody else, everbody had just a very little bit. They'd just get by. The milk and eggs and chickens came off the place, but we'd have to drive eighty miles to Roswell to buy the feed for the stock. And we needed cash for the feed.

Part of the time, we'd go off and work for other ranchers, my husband and I. We worked out from nineteen thirty-three up into the forties. And when you work that way on a ranch, the woman has to cook for the ranch, for her board and room. That's all she gets, just her eats. That's all I was used to. You didn't expect anything better. And, well, my husband just got thirty-five dollars a month for workin ever day. Ridin broncs, gatherin cows, an brandin, anything there was, workin on the windmill, anything at all. That's just how it was.

Christine was born in 1940. My husband and I were married five or six years before we had any children. We didn't have enough money! My husband's mother had eight children, and it kind of got her down; so he helped, he kind of helped me along with not gettin pregnant. That year that Christine was born, we worked for Jimmy Hall that year. And talk about milkin a cow! I was pretty big, I'm short anyhow, and when I was pregnant I was pretty big. I'd go out and milk the cow ever night, an this Mr. Hall that we worked for— we were working for thirty dollars a month, boarding ourselves—Mr. Hall says, "Milt, if you don't get that girl out of that lot, she's going to have that baby milkin that cow!"

An Milt said, "Well, if she can have it that easy, jest let her alone, and I'll bring the baby to the house when it gets here!"

Well, I didn't mind! But it wasn't *quite* that easy. I went fifty miles to Carazozo when my time came. I got in there and Dr. Turner had gone to a *golf* tournament. Well, I didn't know I could have that baby without the doctor!

And Bennie said, "Oh, we'll have it anyway, whether he gets here or not!"

Bennie was the head nurse and I didn't have sense enough to know she knew how to take care of me same as the doctor. I was pretty scared. And she said, well, she wasn't gonna let my husband stay in there with me.

"Well," I said, "then I won't go in that hospital."

And she said, "Well, you will!"

And I said, "No I won't, either. I'll lay right out there on that ground and have that baby with him right there with me. I'd ruther have him than you!"

So she says, "All right then, darn it!" And she let him stay right by the bed and help me.

Must have been after Christine was born that we got the first sheep. Before that, we just worked out for wages, see. Then after we finally got our first start with sheep, well, we never did ever go completely out of the sheep business again until after Milt died.

We had to borry money to live on and borry money for the sheep. Seems like it was seventy-five dollars a month that they would allow us, and that was to buy feed for the stock, and for us to live, and for everthing, for us to take care of *everthing*. And then, see, we'd sell a few lambs and we'd sell the wool, what was it then? About twenty cents a pound, ten cents? We *have* sold wool for ten cents a pound. We kept the best ewe lambs to build up our flock, we couldn't keep them all cause we couldn't afford to, see. We had to pay so much on our note. See, we didn't have *any* money but if we paid enough on it, they'd make us a new note, and then we'd pay the next year, and . . . well, all this time they kept saying, "We're loanin you the money to improve, cause we want you to be able to be self-reliant." The Roswell Production Company, it would loan money mostly to ranchers and farmers. They'd make us out a list, they'd say now you can have so much for groceries, an . . . I think this seventy-five dollars was for everything we had, our gasoline, our coal oil, our—cause, see, we didn't have any lights. And we finally got a radio with a battery, *oh boy!* Did we enjoy ourselves with that!

When the oldest girl started school, the two girls and I moved into town, to Ancho. We didn't have a car or anything. At that time we had just the one pickup, so Milt would take us to there and haul us a barrel of water; we didn't have any water at the house in Ancho, either. That barrel had to last till Milt got back at the end of the week. So I'd bathe the baby in the washtub, then the other little girl, then myself, then mop the floor, out of just one washtub of water!

Ancho was twenty-nine miles from the ranch. We paid five dollars a month for that house. Then on Fridays, Milt would come get us and we'd go back to the ranch. I didn't feel like there was any choice 'bout movin into town. I didn't think I was smart enough to educate my kids. I never went to college, just went through high school. And I thought my kids needed other friends their own age. So we moved on into Ancho. Part of that time, I cooked the school lunches at the schoolhouse to be with the kids. I had to get a job, see, that I could work durin school hours. Leavin my husband, I thought I would *die!* I was very much in *luuuuuuve* with him, I didn't want to leave him. My goodness! I thought that that was awful! Worked out, though. Maybe that's one of the reasons we got along so well, we was gone five days each week. Oh, I think we would have got along together whatever, cause we were married six years before we had any children. And then another six years, see, before Christine started school. So we had twelve years of married life before I had to go into town.

I don't know there was much of anything on this ranch I didn't do, except climb the windmill. I never could climb a windmill. I'd always be lookin up and see a cloud, an try to follow that cloud. My husband said, "You stay on the ground, you're just gonna end up there anyway!"

And I'd go an help him grind the feed. He wouldn't let me grind by myself, though I think I could have. No, there wasn't really anything I didn't at least *try* to do. But it was because my nature was I wanted to see if I *could* do it. I wanted to be a jack-of-all-trades. I think it's good for people. I think men should know how to cook and take care of a house. Sometime in life they might have to, and I think they should know how. And I think the woman should know how to do the work outside.

Course, ranch life is different, you see, you all work together for the same purpose. In town, well like these kiddos, their daddy is a welder and their mother works in the post office. That's different work, completely. So Betty couldn't go weld, and Pat couldn't go work in the post office. It's a different life in town than what I was used to.

In the winters out on the ranch you nearly sat at home all the time, we didn't go very much. We would read, and play cards; we'd play rummy and dominoes, and forty-two. And then we had these checker games, Chinese checkers, we got into that. But I think that's one reason why I got into a lot of crocheting and knitting, and then took up spinning and weaving. Cause that was somethin to do. And I had the piano. My husband could sleep quite a bit during the day, but I never could sleep during the daytime. And we'd always have the stock to take care of, an we could get out and walk around and just enjoy ourselves—mostly it was just the family together.

Cause back then you see, we didn't have a tank on the ranch for gas. We had a fifty-five-gallon barrel, an we had to go into Carazozo, fifty miles, to get this fifty-five-gallon barrel full of gas. Out here, it had to last us for a long time. We made very few trips into town, once a week was the most we ever did. For that reason, we didn't go visitin much either, cause we didn't have the money to go much. Now if we were going to work stock, we made a point for all of us to go and help the neighbors, and they'd all come back to help us sometime. But just to go and visit, we'd very seldom do that. But if somebody needed somethin and they had a neighbor that was closer to them than town, well they'd borry it rather than goin all the way to town.

You very seldom have anybody ask to borry anything from you today, though. I think the times of the world have changed, and then the different people that have come into this area. The younger ones have so much more money to spend than we did too; I can see . . . it isn't so much *them,* as the whole times of the world's changin. And it's hard for me to keep adjusting. I don't think people are as happy now as we were. If you watch TV and you have a program you want to watch on TV, well, I don't want to watch that one, so I fuss at you to watch mine. Well, all we had was the radio—finally we did finally get a radio, see—and we didn't probably have but one or two stations that we could listen at. So we didn't have much choice, you see; that's why I say, "Make the best of what you have." See, we had to *make* our good times out here; we didn't have a lot of entertainment to choose from, we had to *make* what fun we had.

People nowadays have too much to make the best of what they have. And nowadays, the mother can work and when she comes in she can go to one place, and the daddy'll go someplace else, and the kids'll go to the babysitter. But we had a *union,* we had a *family union.* We did things together. We'd both be out here workin sheep. If we worked sheep, we all went out and did it together. Where I think that makes a happier family life, than everyone bein separate.

Lookin back now, I think that maybe Milt made more of the decisions. But at the time, I *thought* I made quite a few of 'em! But I look back now, and he was very quiet. He could make you do what he wanted to without sayin a word. And I'd be goin, "Babababa," thinkin I was gettin my way! But we compromised with each other. If he ever told me no, that was *no* then. But he didn't say it very often. If he'd say, "Oh, I don't know about that," well, I knew I could get around that. But if he said no, well, we didn't do it. Offhand, I can't think of anything he did say *no* about, though.

I think what makes a good marriage is workin together and makin the best of it. And tryin to get along—go a little bit more than fifty-fifty. Milt would give a little in my direction, and the next time, he'd get sixty and I'd get forty. Now, that's in my time of life—these are different times, I don't know what I'd do now, cause I'm not in it personally. . . . You know, you can have happiness if you want to, if you look hard enough for it, most of us. But you may have to have the right one, see; I'm not sayin that everbody'd be happy together. Maybe I was lucky and I did have the right one. I think you have *work* after happiness though, I don't think it's just settin there ready for you to accept. You have to work for it.

We got pleasure in the work that we did, we both loved livestock. I never had been around sheep before I moved here, but I learned to love sheep and our ranch wasn't big enough for cattle, so there's the reason we worked with sheep. Even if it is hard work, if you *like* it, you're happy doin it. Where if you *hate* the work—but there you go again, make the best of whatever you got, even if it isn't what you really like the best. Make the best of it, and you might learn to like it.

There is some that have come out here to work that have never learned to do it right. There has been boys that come out here that I'd say, "Don't you boys want a cup of coffee? Why don't you go on into the house?" Well, I could work those old sheep out there, standin there and talkin to 'em, gettin in the middle of the corral, and directly they'd walk around me and they'd go the way I wanted them to. But these boys would be a hootin and a hollerin an a-takin on so, and scarin the sheep to death. You can't get anything done! Ben Payne told me one time, "To work sheep *fast,* you *work* sheep slow." And that's the truth! Cause you get in a hurry behind an old sheep and she'll go ever way in the world but the right way! And the whole bunch will be sure to run after that one, specially if it's the wrong way!

Oh, I was lucky in my life! I've had a happy life, and I guess that's enough. Milt always said, "Make the best of what you have." I've heard that many a time in my life. Sure, there were times when it was hard. You have to have sorrow and joy too, to make you appreciate the joy. If everthing was perfect, you'd be very unhappy. You wouldn't have a thing to complain about! We didn't have a lot of things. We didn't have everthing to eat like a lot of people do now. We didn't have *everything* we wanted to eat, but we always had somethin to keep going on, you know. We didn't starve. That didn't hurt us. Everybody else did too; they had to do without a few things too. It was learning. I learned to get along with what I had, and to make *good* of it. Say "Okay, we're happy the way we are." We don't have this, we don't have a good car—sure, I wished I had a car when I went into town with the kids. And now, I don't know why I didn't, but I didn't! I bet we could've taken two hundred dollars and bought an old second-hand car that would have lasted forever. But we just never did do it. But still, all in all, we had what we wanted.

I don't worry about gettin old. I know I'll get older, yes. I'm sixty-six years old. But as long as I can keep goin, same old two feet . . . but when that time comes, why I hope I go to a rest home. I don't want to live with my daughters. Nope. Different generations, generation gap. I firmly believe in the generation gap, cause I have had older women with me when I was young. When my kids were smaller than these granddaughters here, there was an old lady that lived by me. And I can remember, she would come to see me on the hottest day, like today, and I was young and I was dressed like you girls are with the thin blouses on, and she would sit there with the long-sleeved dress and a sweater. I liked to burn up just lookin at her! And she'd say, "Kind of cool, ain't it?"

So your generation gap—two women cain't live in the same house with the young kiddos that are so energetic, have a lot of body heat. . . . I would be cold all the time, I cain't eat like the younger generation can . . . everthing is so *different*. Now, if somethin happens that I *have* to live with my children, I would want one corner, where I can go in there and keep it as hot or as cold, or whatever I want in there, and be out of their way. But no, I wouldn't live with them, less one of them is sick and needs me, or somethin where we'd have to. But I want them to live their lives. I lived mine, and had a pretty good time, too.

I don't think you feel the generation gap with your own family as long as they are your responsibility. It's when they get married and have a family of their own is when it seems like the worst gap is between us. Because when they're young and growin up, they are *yours* to take care of, they are *your* responsibility. But when they have a family of their own, well, then you sort of feel *old,* or somethin. When they're growin up, you're young enough to be with them and get along and do about as much as they do. Whereas these grandkids here, I cain't keep up with them, but I could with my own kids.

Now this granddaughter, she's fifteen years old. She doesn't have a boy friend.

She says, "Oh, I like them all, but who I really like is my *horse!*"

The little one likes horses too, but I believe the older one—she's always said, "Nana, what are you goin to do with the ranch? If I ever get married, I sure wish I could go out there and live!"

When You Have To Do, You'll Do

Lillian Fox

Lillian Fox lives in the mountains of Western North Carolina. Her house, a gray stone cottage, sits nestled in a mountain "holler." When spring comes, the hollow is so green it almost hurts your eyes. Lillian's house is set in a rainbow of color, as huge flower gardens circle round it. Beyond the flower beds are vegetable patches large enough to feed a small army. And everywhere I looked, I saw care and vision mingled to produce beauty.

I'm seventy years old. Some people just won't believe that I'm that old, but I tell them I can show them the old family Bible. There were thirteen in our family. I was in the middle. At first there was two years between the children and then with the last five or six, there was three years between them. My mother bore children for thirty-two years, thirteen children. After a child was born, as soon as it got, you know—well, it didn't have to be very old—she would go out in the fields. It would nurse the breast—you know all of them did that back then—she would let it nurse on her before she'd go out to the fields in the morning and then when she'd come back at night. She'd rather have worked outside than in. She said she missed me awful when I left home. Well, I was the oldest girl left to home and I helped with the little ones. She'd never had a daughter stay till she was twenty years old before, they'd all married when they was about seventeen. She said she missed me terrible when I left home. She never did have to tell me what to do or anything around the house.

I got married in nineteen twenty-nine, when I was twenty years old. Virgil Fox, that was my husband. We lived down in Marshall for two years and then came up here; I've lived here ever since. I had two children, a boy and a girl. My husband went in the Navy when our son was just small and he came back changed. He didn't care nothin about the home, or me, or the kids after that. So my brothers helped me build this house. I'd saved enough money while he was gone in the service to do it. All this paneling came off of the place. I had the timber cut and dried. Yes, I saved to build it. Course, my brothers laid the rock; if they hadn't, I couldn't have done it. *I* like it. There's a lot of people that wanted me to move away, but I'm gonna be here long as I can go at all. It gets pretty hard sometimes, but . . .

I sold this place one time and in two weeks, just a little over two weeks, I lost fourteen pounds. I couldn't eat, I couldn't sleep or anything. The night this woman came back to see me, she asked me what was wrong and I told her I couldn't eat or sleep or nothin else just thinkin about sellin this.

And she said, "Miz Fox, I really want it, but if it means that much to you, you can have it back."

And I said then, that unless it was a have-to case, I'd never sell this place. I don't guess it hurts everyone alike, you know. But I put so much into it. The gardens, and all the paneling, and sheetrocking in here. I'd never seen any sheetrock filled, nobody showed me how to do it, I just did. I started one week and got it all done the next week. And then I took rheumatoid arthritis, oh my legs was all swelled up and bruised and discolored, you know. I didn't walk for three months. That was after I did all the paneling and finishing on this house. They say that's when I caught it in my nerves. No, I haven't had a very easy life.

My husband, he pretended to be here. But he never was here very much. How do you reckon I clothed my kids and sent them to school? Pickin galax. Fifty cents a thousand branches. You put twenty-five branches in a bunch and it took forty bunches. I could usually get five or six thousand in a day. Course, back then, that was a little more money! But my daughter, she wouldn't wear a dress I'd bought at the store. I had to make all her clothes. No, she wouldn't wear anything bought. I didn't mind the sewin, but I had so much to do.

This gettin up at four o'clock and workin till ten or eleven at night . . . it gets to ya . . . I always had two cows to milk, chickens to feed, hogs to feed, the field crops to raise. The reason I had to get up at four o'clock was that I had to do the mendin, and the ironin, and the washin before I'd get the breakfast. And then at night, I'd have the sewin and all that work to do too. I did all the cookin on a wood stove. I ain't had an electric stove I'd guess but about ten year. An I did all the washin on a board. And I hauled all my water from the spring. My daughter helped me some, but she married afore she was seventeen. She got married to get away from her daddy. Otherwise, I don't believe she'd have left. Leastways, not so soon.

I had the whole bottom in corn too, and then I had a real big garden, sames as I do now. My daddy would plow for me and then I'd go help him, sames as he'd helped me. Oh, mercy! When my husband was in service, his parents brought J. D. Winkler out here electioneerin one time. He was mayor in Haysville, you know. And J.D. says to my husband's daddy, "Well, I think Virgil just better stay away," he says, "if his wife can keep a place a lookin like this! It looks a lot better than I ever seen it."

And after I'd done all that and worked all year an got my crop in, my husband would come and take it to town and sell it. An I never seen the money. So then one year, my daddy said, "Lillian, I'll tidy you a potato patch over in my field over yonder. Then he can sell the patch you have here but you'll still have some for you and the children."

So he give me the seed to plant over there too, and I raised that crop. And when I got it home, my husband took and sold it too. Oh, my husband worked, but he didn't spend the money here. I lived with him nearly thirty year and he didn't buy *anything,* not a sheet, towel, pillowcase, nothin, *ever.* He bought my daughter just one dress in all the time till she graduated from school. I sold galax, and then I'd sell eggs, you know, and vegetables out of the garden too. People still come from as far away as Haysville to get my eggs.

I don't know how I learned to do all I did. I had never planted anything, never grew anything, till after I was married. It's like one time I had the cow staked in this real tall grass down in the meadow. And my dad was way over yonder plowin at my uncle Anders' place. And the cow got choked, and I sent one of the kids after my daddy, you know. But I seen that cow was gonna die afore he got there, cause it was a good ways over to there. So I took a handful of salt and I put it as far down her throat as I could and she got all right. She'd got a big wad of grass stuck in her throat and I knew that salt would form a saliva, you know. And she was okay and kicking when my daddy got here.

"I couldn't have done any better myself," he said.

Oh, there's a lot of ways to do, when you have to. When you have to do, you'll do. You see, I don't have anybody I can depend on. *Nobody* . . .

I've lived alone twenty years, it'll be twenty-one next January. We was married in twenty-nine and my husband left in fifty-nine. My daughter was married by then and my son'd went off to work. It was a relief when my husband left. It was a relief, honey child. Lord have mercy! You see that scar there? That's where he knocked me against a rock out there and my daddy says, "I think you done killed her this time." He broke my glasses all up and he hit my daddy. He injured my spine. I've got a scar there. No, it was a *relief* when he left.

His mother said I was too good to him. And *my* mother said maybe if I was real good to him, he'd change his ways. Naw, but he beat me, and he beat my son terrible, and the cows, anything that lived. He finally almost broke that arm, cracked it.

And I told him one day, I said, "If you ever hit me agin, I'll pay you back. If'n I have to wait till you went to sleep, I'll pay you back."

He knew I meant it, and he left. I did mean it too. I'd had all I could take.

He whupped our son one time until there was blood. And he

made him straddle that chair and he poured alcohol in them cuts. Lord, when that boy was a child, he'd get to beating him and I'd try to pull him off of him, and he'd just knock me over.

No, when he cut my chin, that scar there, and I was bruised all over, I took out papers for it. And everbody around here, they all said they didn't have no idea that he done like that to me. Well, I never did believe in, well you know, tellin everbody about your troubles. Mr. Sam Williams was out mowin briars one day an I was out hoein corn and my husband was a-beatin me, and Mr. Sam saw him. So that time when I indicted him, my husband asked Mr. Sam to be a charACKter witness.

And Mr. Sam told him, "I won't do it. I know what you done to her."

And then sometime later, Mr. Sam was a-talkin and he says, "Lillian, I don't know how you've stood it as long as you have. God Almighty couldn't get along with Virgil Fox."

But when we went to court that old Stacy Smith was the one that said that I was so bruised up because I fell down all the time and bruised real easy. *My* husband paid him to say that to the jury. He paid the jury too, to say he wasn't guilty. The old judge leaned down and said, "I know you're guilty, and you know you're guilty, but the jury says you're not, so I've got to let you go." My husband set right here and owned up to me, said it took him over a year to pay that jury off.

I couldn't get a divorce. The judge told me, "We know he's guilty, but jury says he's not and there's nothin I can do."

When I took out them papers I was just tryin to get it fixed some way so's he couldn't never beat me agin. But the jury just let him go. That's why I didn't try agin. You know that money and a big name can do most anything. If anybody's got money, they can get what they want.

Well I had a lot of flowers, but not as many as I do now, before he left. Because he wouldn't let me work in that flower garden. He'd raise Cain if I did while he's there. Only time I'd get to work in the flowers was when it was too wet to work in my garden. But after I'd raised my garden, he'd take my vegetables off and sell them. I know I told him one time not to take any more beans off, I wanted to can some for us to have in wintertime. And he went out there and picked them off in the moonlight. No, people wouldn't believe how he was, unless they'd seen it.

But flowers was the one thing he couldn't sell.

I got into gardening cause I had to. We had to eat something. But I did the flowers just cause I wanted to. Couple years before my husband left, he went off one mornin. Now the cows was mine, but he went off one mornin and he said if when he come back, I'd staked that cow anywhere on this place, he'd cut her up. Well, I was worried to death. An then this Miz Craven come by, and she'd seen my flowers afore and wanted some bulbs to set out. Well, I give her just a small bag and she give me a ten-dollar bill. Well, Mr. Sam Williams that owned that field over there, come by just then and I told him about my husband. And he said I could put my cow over in his field, and I give him that ten-dollar bill. Those was the first flowers I ever sold.

And many a time, I've thought how that worked out. That she'd come an buy them dahlia bulbs, and then that Mr. Sam would come by and rent me that pasture. And that ten-dollar bill was the only money I had in the world! I had that cow in Mr. Sam's pasture afore my husband come back.

Oh, he was cruel! He'd tie the cow out there so's she couldn't put her head down. Couldn't eat or drink and she was nursin a calf. An he beat two cows till they lost their calves. An then you ask me if I was sorry to see him go? Well, my daughter says there was bound to be somethin wrong with his brain.

The last time I seen him, must have been twelve years ago. He'd been to his cousin's funeral and I was workin out there on my flowers right next to the fence. And he didn't come on the inside.

He says, "It hurt Tessie"—that was his cousin—"awful bad when Ball"—that's her husband—"died."

And I says, "It hurts any woman when her husband dies, or any man for his wife to die. But," I says, "the main thing is how they've treated them while they've lived with them." I says, "My conscience is clear about you. But," I says, "I wonder if I die first if you'll think about that scar on my chin, or my spine where you injured it, or my wrist where you cracked it."

And he just picked up and left. That was the last I ever saw of him. But I *do* believe that, I believe that's the reason it hurts some people when other people die, it's because of the way they've treated them.

No, I never did think of leavin here. I just kept hopin he'd leave. I'd worked too hard to have this place. I'd saved for it, and I'd made it what it was. I saved that money by bein careful . . . *real careful*. . . . Lot of people now says they don't see how in the world I get by, but I learned early to be careful. He never gave me anything. A lot of folks says I'm awful hardhearted. I don't wish him no harm, but I don't never want to see him agin. An I was *glad* when he left, real glad.

I've been alone almost twenty-one years now. I like bein by myself. I do. That's one reason I don't visit my sisters and brothers more. I stay one night and it seems like I've been gone a month and I just want to come back home. They've been after me to get somebody to stay with me, look after me, especially after I broke my hip. But I say, as long as somebody can get by, they had an easier time alone than with somebody with 'em. Because when you're hungry you can fix yourself somethin. You can go to bed when you want and get up when you want. If'n there's somebody here, it's not that way. I like for people to visit—and sometimes I'm pretty glad to see them leave, too!

I was in the seventh grade when I quit school. Back then, there wasn't many that went past that. Well, I'll tell you, I can't write good at all, but I can write better than one of my brothers' wives, and she finished high school! An I like to read. I think I've read thirty books in the last month. Sometimes on Sundays, I kin get two read. I tell everbody that's my nerve medicine. The doctor gave me them pills to take. But if I kin just read a while afore I go to bed, it settles my nerves so's I don't need them pills. Course I got cataracts now, and there's times I can't see to read but them easy-print books.

I usually have pansies out there, an carnations. Then there's a row of gladiolas, then two rows of calla lilies, an a row of peacock orchids. Then a hunderd an four hills of dahlias. I've got pansies I've had, oh Lord, ever since I've lived here, since nineteen thirty-one, and they'll keep seedin themselves. But the plants you buy nowadays, they'll die. I reckon they're highbred. And I've got corn and beans that I've had ever since I come here too. My mother gave me the seed and I've saved it every year since.

I had a real good garden the summer after I broke my hip in February. I planted part of it when I was still on the walker. I don't know how I done that. I set out my onions, sowed my lettuce, things like that, while I was still on the walker. I had a real good garden that summer.

And that girl that was givin me therapy, she said, "Now if you *have* to work in that garden, you set in a chair."

Now, wouldn't I have got a lot done, settin in a chair? And one time she come to see me and I'd picked a bushel of butter beans and a bushel of them green beans.

And she said, "Did you pick them settin in your chair?"

Now, how could I have picked them beans from a chair? When the butter beans, some of 'em, run six feet high?

I've got so many ailments and each one aggravates the other. But I don't notice the hurtin if I'm able to get outside and work. Course, I have to walk with a stick outside—that, or lean on my hoe. But sometimes those muscles gets so they just won't work. They're too short, from the operation. I know one time when I was cleanin out them weeds back in October, an I worked out there bendin over till I like not to have got back to the house. It just won't work when I bend over too long. But workin helps, don't it? You don't notice the pain when you can get out there and work.

So many people comes here and says, "Well, who does your yard work? Who tends your gardens?"

An I says, "I DO."

A Different Way of Looking
Myra Grant

Myra Grant lives with her husband, Lyle, on a dairy farm in Sanger-
ville, Maine, in the center of the state. She is forty-one and has five
children, three of whom still live at home. Like many farm women
today, Myra works in town to bring in needed cash income to supple-
ment what the farm produces.

When first approached about an interview, she said, "Oh, you
don't want to talk to me, all I've got to say is that farmin's too hard a
life." Our talk, as it turned out, was an exploration for both of us of
the trials and joys of that way of life.

I was born in Garland, which is just about ten miles from here. I
called it a farm because we had one cow, chickens, pigs, running
around. But we didn't milk forty cows and ship milk like we do
here. . . . Well, I was one of sixteen children. Two sets of twins in the
family, I have a twin brother. There is thirteen living children now,
three of them died within two years of birth. I'm the next to the last.

My father was crippled, he was taken with the infantile paralysis. And back then they didn't have the medication which they have now, so I never seen him walk. When I look back to then, I sometimes think I wish I could just turn times back, because, well, it seems like people were *closer*. Back then, if one neighbor needed help, you didn't give it a thought, you just helped them. Seems though in recent years it's "You pay me first, then I'll do it."

I went to a one-room schoolhouse where all eight grades were there. If I remember right there was eight graduated from the grammar school my year. I'm not sure how many is in a high school class now, but it is some different from then! You know, the way the school was back then. I remember a wood stove settin there, you'd have to huddle around that to keep warm or we'd keep hot rocks to put our feet on. It's a considerable difference from what they do now. It's been quite a change. I can remember back then, they had programs where parents and children were more involved than they are today. I suppose they have more—what would I say?—activities for the children now. But back then they would have PTA—well, they do *now,* but it's different, to get parents involved *now,* a lot of them say, "Take my kids, get them out of my hair." Which I don't approve of. And I can remember back in the grammar school, they'd put on *plays,* and *everyone* would be involved. In that small community—well now they've combined all the schools and they bus all the children—but *then* in West Garland, everybody knew their neighbors, knew who lived in what house, practically knew their whole business! I mean, it was all *one,* just one small community.

I often think I wonder how my mother and father ever raised sixteen children—well, I should say thirteen, I guess. And then they had two boys that didn't have a home or family that lived there with us too. It was just a natural thing, they were just considered one of the family. But I have five children, and I wonder how would I ever manage with thirteen of them! I remember Mother on washdays, she had an old gas washing machine set out in a shed, we had *lines* of clothes. I don't know many women that could stand that now. In winter, we'd hang them out in the shed, couldn't hang them outdoors cause they would just freeze. She didn't have a dryer—my mother never even had a bathroom. We always had what was called an outhouse in the shed. And after we were all grown up, let's see, we *all* had left home before she ever had a bathroom. Most of the places around here were like that, very few had indoor flushings or bathrooms or anything like that. We always had to run down and keep warm in front of the wood fire to take our baths, and everybody would clear out of one room. It was just our natural thing! I've often wondered, I'd like to see if I could do it nowadays! But it was quite a way of life. I *enjoyed* it.

I don't know to think back that I had any certain jobs. Course we had our rooms that we had to keep clean. And we'd be out around when they were hayin, and just—I don't know, we just helped out, we just *knew* that we should help out and we just never had to be told. There were certain things that had to be done. A few years, my folks raised string beans, when there was a cannery in Dexter. And they would hire so many kids to pick beans, and I remember us going out to pick beans. We would save our money, we were allowed to use our money for whatever we wanted to. I remember my twin brother and I wanted a wheel for a bicycle and we saved our money to get it. But we went to town and they didn't have the right one, so I came back with a skirt. And my father teased me some, thought that was the *funniest-lookin* bicycle wheel he ever saw!

I don't know. I enjoyed it. I still enjoy farmin. But *it's—a lot of—hard work.* I don't know as I can really say I enjoy it, because sometimes I think it's *too* much hard work. When we first started farmin here, we lived in the house down below and Lyle's folks had this farm. Well, they got so they couldn't farm it, but they didn't want to sell it to us.

They said, "You work here, and we'll give it to you."

But we couldn't do that. We wanted to buy it. So, we just rented the barn. And Lyle was drivin milk truck days and I was workin in a little grocery store that was in Dover, and we had the five children that was in school. So it was quite a—quite a battle. And if there was a sick cow, well I worked for a *fantastic* lady and she'd give me a little extra time off. At noontime, I'd rush home, tend to my clothes, rush out to the barn, doctor the cow—I might have to call up a neighbor to come help me hold the cow—*and* go back to the house, clean up, and get back to work! He was drivin milk truck and I guess I got a little down on farmin *then,* because when I worked myself, trying to carry on two jobs, I didn't know enough to stop. That was my own problem: I know I'm to blame on that myself. But actually three jobs, with the children too, and the store, and the farm. And if the children were sick, well I'd call in, because you know, I wouldn't go in if they were sick. This woman with the store, she was a fantastic person to work for—not many would be that understanding.

In winter we've been known to be, oh not too often, but we've been known to be in here three for four days with no way out. But that doesn't bother me. That's a minor thing! You expect that, and I suppose that's the price you pay for livin out of town. But I don't believe that I could *ever* be content in town. There's so much traffic and commotion! I don't mind goin to the city to visit, but to *live* . . . all that noise. And I wonder, "How do people keep their *sanity,* really?" When my relatives in Massachusetts came up to visit us the first time, it's so quiet here that my brother's wife, she was just bout afraid! But now they just love it. They'll bring their camper and camp out down by the farm pond. That's where I go a lot of days in summer. If I don't have anything to do, I'll just go down there by the quiet, and it's—peaceful . . . and it's beautiful here, when the snow begins to go and you look out across, and see the deer beginning to come out. We've had Canadian geese settle on the pond too. I guess what I love about it here is that it is so peaceful and quiet. If I want to be alone, I don't have to go too far!

And I wouldn't be content to not live on a farm. It didn't bother me to move out of the new house that we built down below and to move up here, but if I had to move out of this place, I *would* be upset! And as I told my husband and the boys, if you want to farm, *fine,* but I had better work out and bring a *little* income that way! And I think everyone needs a little added income. It took me a *long* while, I wasn't sure I could work out among the public. I'm just not that *forgoing,* but I found that I can, so . . . I knew if I ever *had* to I could, but . . . The store was the first time. I'm not sure that I would have gone right ahead but I had a relative that worked there, and she asked if I—and I thought, "Oh, I've *never* done anything like that." But once after the first week, I was fine and I enjoyed it, meeting new people, and I think it helped me immensely. Because I had never—I'd just been a homebody and a farm wife and just never . . .

I had a previous marriage. I quit school when I was seventeen— and I look back and I wonder *why* my parents ever let me. It wasn't a have-to marriage, *but* we were married about six years and then that came to an end. And the oldest boys were two and three when I divorced. When I got married again, Lyle adopted the boys, which I think was really a great help to them, because—everybody will say, "Oh, divorce don't bother children," but I don't care *how* little, they can feel the tension and everthing.

Lyle was born in Garland, he's ten years older than I am and went to the schools, but he didn't go to the same school at the same time as I did. I never met him, until after my divorce. Which is funny. But when I think of it, I say, "Yes, but when I was born he was ten years old." But I met him here in Dover through a friend. It's been—it's been a *good* marriage.

I had a house which we moved to here after we got married. And then what year was it? I was expecting my last child when we got burned out, down below here, back in sixty-five. And that was—we none of us was home, and thank goodness it didn't happen at night-time! I had gone to Dexter to visit my sister and someone contacted me there and explained that our house had burned. And I was just—I can't *explain*—all we had left was just *the clothes on our backs!* It was *just* . . . And the children didn't sleep good! We had a barn there that we had animals in, but we moved them out of it and had it all boarded up so when you stepped in, there was a stove and a refrigerator on one end and on the other end was a bed. So you either went in and you set down at a plank to eat on, or you had a bed to crawl into! At that time, we had just the four little ones. All of our relatives, friends, neighbors, helped board that up. But the children, even though they weren't there when the house burned, they'd wake up in the night seein that flame. It was months afterwards before they could rest in peace.

But we rebuilt the house. In fact, we laid the whole cement foundation on one terrible hot day. It must have been a hundred degrees pouring that cement floor. But we did it, so that when my last child was born, we were livin in the cellar and we had one bedroom finished off upstairs, so when I came home with the little fella, I could move in there. We built that house all ourselves, my husband and I. In fact the ceiling in the living room, he put that up while he was sick from his job with flu! He'd work a little while and then lay back down. When I think of buildin a house, I don't know if I would want to do it again. We enjoyed it, but it's a loooooong time of gettin it done. We never did completely finish it. We had a chance to buy this, so we sold that. I did just about everything from putting up two-by-fours, to ceilings, you name it! I got up to help shingle cause he put me in the bucket to get me up! I could go *up* the ladder all right, but it was comin back down, tryin to get around the edge of the roof, pregnant like that—so he hauled me up and down in the bucket. Helpin with the chimney, you name it. I did all the painting and wallpapering. That and putting the wallboard in, matching the seams, sanding all that down, I didn't think I would ever get that all done! It wasn't a professional job, far from it but—! And I swirled my own ceilings. And just a *lot* of backbreaking work. And I always thought, "Oh you'd hate to leave a house you built," and I really thought I would, but I didn't. Because this house, his family had always lived here.

I did work out in the barn when we first came up here. We all work helping out in the barn. I'd go out and help with the milking.

Sometimes if he had things to do, I'd go out and clean out the manure —that's when we used a wheelbarrow and then had to take it out into the manure shed! But I was tryin to do two jobs and I just wore myself down. And the doctor told me not to work out in the barn. If I would just know enough to stop, but I just wanted to help out so much I just kept goin. And anyway, I don't mind the farm work. I *love* to be able to go out and deliver a calf!

We're at thirty milkers now, with the dry ones just startin to have calves and comin back. We'd like to be at forty milkers, that would give us a good income. Really, you need to, with the boys workin, because they get a percentage of the milk. It's not that high of a percentage right now, but we figure they need a percentage to give them the incentive to do good work around the cows. Because the better their work is, the better the cows are goin to produce. And we're shippin about two thousand pounds of milk every other day, which isn't that great, but for a small farm is pretty good. We have three hundred acres here, it's two hundred in woods and a hundred in cleared land. We get our hay off of it. And if the boys are really interested . . . We told them that they'll have to work for what they have, cause we're not turnin everything over to them! We've had to work, and to pay quite a bit for the farm, even though it was bought through family members. But sometimes I think you find that it's harder to deal with relatives than it is with friends!

Lyle and the neighbor work back and forth, he likes to have Lyle plant his corn and harvest it, and in return, we use his equipment. I don't know if an arrangement like we have with neighbors is common anymore. Danny Herd is an exceptional fella. We're really lucky, because I think all the neighbors on this road are very good. They'll do anything to help out. The neighbors on this road are very quick to come to anyone's aid. In fact, the chicken farm up the road, those folks, the Risotellos, came here from New York. And one day before we moved into this house, we came up and we were going to shovel off the barn roof because there was a lot of snow on it. How we were going to shovel it off, I wasn't sure. But I said we'd better do it, because we knew . . . Well we came up and we stepped into that barn and those cows just flew right up off of that floor. It sounded just like corn poppin, we could hear the timbers in that barn roof, *cracking*. You could see the timbers just splitting apart. And we didn't have a ladder that would get up there, so we called the Fire Department. And the sheriff's department came out with the jailees, and they would have gone up, but Lyle said no, he couldn't allow it. So we turned the cows loose and the firemen put the ladders up, and you could see that roof just sagging. And the neighbors—Risotellos—came down, he and his brother, and those were the only two fellas who would go up on that roof with my husband. And I don't know how many tons they shoveled because it must have been at least three feet deep up there, and that barn is one hundred feet long. And then another neighbor, Roland Cookson, came and helped—nobody else dared to go up there and we couldn't blame them, timbers were just splitting. But they got the snow off, and if they hadn't that barn would have come down, and I don't know how we would have ever replaced it . . . but it was just like corn poppin and I knew something was wrong, because the minute I opened the door, the cows were just all uneasy.

So the neighbors *really*—and these weren't all neighbors from around here either, as I say—Risotellos had moved in from New York and they stayed right in there with Lyle till they got it done, and I'm tellin you, that was a lot of snow to shovel! I feel there are good and bad in out-of-staters, just like there are in our people. I've *never* been against out-of-staters. I suppose when it comes hunting time, I've been ill at ease, because I've seen a few . . . But to me, given a chance, there's good and bad in all *us* too. And all the neighbors on this road, really there isn't one of us that isn't willing to help others out. Like if someone's gone, one of us will take care of their place, and we'll all keep an eye out if we see strange cars on the road. It's just a neighborly thing to do, a *natural* thing, I think.

Back with my folks, there wasn't so many new inventions, no television, and they would set playing cards and games with the children, which now you don't see. The kids'll be watching television or goin into town to the movies or something like that. But back then we made up our *own* games. Course, we didn't have to worry about who you were going to fight and play with, either. "We have our own little neighborhood," my folks used to say! Now, I can remember neighborhoods getting together and having cookouts. When you was haying, you was always having picnics. Nowadays, there's days with that TV, I just think I'll take a *screwdriver* to it.

But to think back to the way it was back then, the families were just closer knit, closer tied, than the families today. A lot of them—I'm not sayin all of them—because I feel my own family is really close knit. I feel that we are *here*. Because I feel that if you can't take time to sit down and listen to your children, and they listen to you, then you should have thought of that before you had them! And they grow up so fast once they start school now, they just—it's, well I realize there's so much they *have* to learn. But once they start school, seems like you've almost *lost* them, because they're so busy and there's so many activities at school, and the drugs and alcohol, that—oh!—back when I was growin up, we'd never even *heard* of!

I hardly ever saw my father have a drink, maybe if an old friend would come by. But it's like an everyday occurrence when some of my friends and relatives from out of state come up, all they do is have a drink in their hands. How *do* they? But to them, it's just a natural thing, they go on vacation, that's their way of relaxin, I guess, but boy if I did that, I'd be out of the picture! I realize it's their way of un-winding, and who's to say they shouldn't? Because it's their lives, you know. I guess that's the difference in life-style, I couldn't *stand* the fast pace. And I suppose that they think they couldn't stand the pace around here, either! The days that I need to get unwound, I'll tell you, if I can get the time, I go down to my sister's in Dexter that has eight kids. You can be down and so discouraged, and I don't care what mood, you'd never find her complaining or unhappy. I go down there and sit and talk, or we'll go shopping, and just being with her will do *wonders* for me. I suppose there's a lot of pressures around here, but we always find a way to work things out. Oh, I worry, but not like I used to. "Where there's a will, there's a way," my father always used to say. And I find that's true: stick with it long enough, and you're going to pull through. I'm more at ease . . . and if things do get too uptight— But to grab a drink! I don't know, it doesn't *solve* anything! Once that's gone, well then you're right back!

Well, I don't know. When somebody says "farmin," I say, "Well, they're crazy to farm, cause it's a lot of hard work!" But then I stop and think, my husband and children have got to be happy in what they do. Why should they be out at a nine-to-five job, if they're not happy? And I'm content. We may not have a lot of expensive material things, but we get a lot of love and happiness and family. And to me, after one bad marriage, it means a lot! An if we have troubles or problems, well, we work them out. I think any family goes through that at times. I really—I don't know what we *would* do, if we weren't farmin. He's not a man to work in a mill, any more than *I* am. I think I would go *crazy* in a closed-up place like that!

I get up about four-thirty. Lyle calls the oldest boy to get up and go out and help do chores. After that, Lyle has his breakfast and I have mine, and I leave for work about six-thirty. My daughter will get the kids' breakfasts before they go to school. And I'm done about two, so I'm home and I have time during the day. I have a big garden to keep up, and there's always work to do outside. My daughter's in basketball and track, so I'll come home and get supper started and then go back to town and pick her up. I try to have supper about five. But that's one thing around here, meals aren't at a certain time! Suppertime may be anywhere, because if you're haying, you may get supper at ten o'clock at night.

My sister-in-law comes up here and she says, "How do you know when to do it?"

Well, after so long, it's just a natural thing. And I may get breakfast on the table and it'll be too early and the eggs get cold, so I just start all over again. You know, I can more or less adjust. If I'm not workin, I don't get up quite this early, I like to sleep longer, but right about six o'clock, I'll realize it's time to start the coffee.

I used to try to get more done before I'd go off to work, but that's something I try not to let bother me. I used to think "Oh, people'd come in and the house would be such a mess." But now I think, if they're comin to visit me, it has to be *me*. And if they don't come back,

I'll know it was my house! I *try* not to let that upset me—it used to considerably, because I *dislike* housework, I would *much* rather be out around outdoors. My husband's mother lived in this house, and everything was just *so;* certain day, she'd wash, certain day, she'd bake, certain day, she'd iron. And I can remember just before her goin, she said, "If I had it to do over again, when my husband wanted me outside, I'd go!" And when I get the chance, if I want to go to the garden or the pond, I go. Let the housework go. For some reason, the housework never disappears, it's always waiting right there! There's more to life than havin a clean house, and as long as we're all healthy and happy, that's the main thing.

I quit high school when I was a sophomore to get married. *Why,* I don't know, and why my parents ever let me, I don't know. Then I went back to school when I first was farmin, and I was takin three night courses a week. One was math, and one was bookkeeping. And believe you me, I'm glad I had such an understanding husband, because I could spend all day on that bookkeeping. I never in my life realized it was so difficult! And if I'd get a sandwich and throw it at them, he'd know where I was—bookkeepin! I wouldn't advise anyone to try three subjects again. I had four kids at the time. No, I had all five kids then. Now, I've got just one credit to go till I graduate; I have all my required credits and when I can just find the time . . . I tell the kids, "Go now." It sounds so simple to think later you'll be old and smarter, but that habit of sitting down and concentrating and studying isn't as easy as it was back then. And I just kick myself that I didn't finish. I tell the kids, *"Please,* take the opportunity to learn what you can while you're young."

My oldest boy quit. He and a girl had to get married—"had to," I shouldn't use that word because there's no such thing. I wasn't sure it was the right thing but she was expecting and we allowed it. But right now, that's over. She had twins and she's found someone else and she's happy. And he's found someone. They're not married, but I'm all for it. It's their own private life. You look around . . . at first I wondered what I did wrong. But no, I said, "I did the best I can." I'm *not* blamin myself, *that* I won't do. If the kids don't . . . I suppose we all feel our kids should turn out a certain way, but I can see so many parents feel their kids ought to be *theirs*. BUT they've got to be their own person.

Maybe my parents could have talked me out of that marriage, but in a way I think I had to go through that mistake, to have the life and the happiness in marriage that I know now. What I had in the first one —there's just no comparin. I had to learn to realize and cherish all I have now. And it hasn't all been my doin, because I have a fantastic husband. I'm not the easiest person to get along with. And I still say, with farming you have the time for the closeness and the honesty. That's one thing, we never had any money at home, but that's one thing our father always drove home.

"If you don't have your honesty, what do you have?" he said.

I've always felt if I could get that across to my own kids . . . Lyin I just can *not* comprehend. I just see *red* when people lie. I don't see how people can *face* one another, if they lie to 'em or cheat 'em. I never was brought up that way, and I remember my father did something when they planted beans, field beans. The field man used to come around and my father would tell how honest his workers were.

"Oh, no," the man said.

"All right," my father said, "I'll prove somethin to you. I put a penny over in one of those kids' envelopes, and you give them fifteen minutes walkin down the road, and they'll be back."

"Oh no, they won't!"

Well, that boy came back and he said, "Mr. Haskell, you gave me too much money, you gave me a penny too much."

That field man had to apologize right there. And that's one thing I always felt was worth more than anything money can buy, is the honesty and love between a family. And I think that's really what you can get out of farmin. You're not going to get rich. You may have a lot of *income*, but it's always got a place to *go*. But I don't want to be rich.

I think my kids are gettin the same kind of values I grew up with. Perhaps not quite so . . . down-to-earth . . . because of the changes in the times, but I hope we've gotten through *some* down-to-earth values. I feel they are much more . . . *prepared* . . . than if they were in town. When I see some of the children in town that don't have anything to do, and I'm sure they're goin to have to work for a livin someday, it's not going to be *handed* to 'em. They don't know about work as kids. But it's not like that on a farm. Sometimes our kids wonder when they do get time off! Oh, not really. Summertime, our camper sits down by the pond and we'll go spend the night down there, camp out. We really enjoy it. There's a certain amount of work to do, but I'll cook lunch down there, and they'll all come down. It's nice that we don't even have to travel to have a good camp-out!

Yes, farmin's a lot of hard work, and sometimes you could just *scream*, but I guess you'd feel that with any job. And we've always had anything that we could want. We always figure that there's a way of havin what you really want. Farming gives you a different way of looking at good times and bad times, a way of attacking the problems and seeing them through. There would have been times, I'm sure, that if I hadn't had the experience of farming I would just have thrown my hands up and given up! There's—you're so totally *involved* in farmin, you can't, if you come up against something, just give up . . . You've got too much to lose. Not just material things either . . . There's just too much *value* there, so that you value— And you can just see so much, so much *achievement,* and so much—oh! what's the word I want to use?—well, once you've worked hard and you've seen so much results from all your hard work, after you've seen *that,* everything's worthwhile, farming.

Well, You Jest Never Know
Jaunita Sultemeier

Jaunita and Clintie Sultemeier are the epitome of a hospitableness that I found only in New Mexico, perhaps for the simple reason that the countryside there is so wide open and the visitors are few. Their ranch consists of fifteen sections, eighteen thousand acres of land, on which they run about eight hundred sheep, plus a smaller herd of cattle. The area is vast, but the desert conditions there are such that it takes ten times as much land to support each animal as it does in more arable regions.

When I first arrived, Jaunita exclaimed, "I didn't know you raised sheep. I didn't know you were that kind of person! Do you want to see some sheep being sheared?" So we hopped in the car and roared off over a one-lane dirt road across empty countryside, seventeen miles to the next neighbor's shearing pens. Such excursions are nothing in a country where it is a forty-mile ride to get the mail in Corona, the nearest town.

Though living in such isolation would be lonely to most people, Jaunita says she has never found it so. She describes her family as a "clan," and after two days seemed to have added me as an honorary second cousin.

Really, the one you ought to be talkin to about me is my mother. Well, I imagine I was a lively little rat, the way she tells it. I have one sister, Oveda, and we grew up I guess you might say kind of like twins, because she was eighteen months older than I was and we went through school the whole time in the same grade. I always lived out in the country, except for a few years when we lived in El Paso; but besides that, I've always been in the country. We did at one time have a little ranch over north of Corona, here, and my daddy mostly went in for horses. At one time, he had over a hundred head of horses, he also had a big herd of angory goats there.

Back in Oklahoma, it was farmland; we had cotton, and the maize, and corn. It was all dry land farmin, and the Dust Bowl is what put us out of Oklahoma. My mother worked in the fields and they had us a workin out in the fields too. I can remember pickin the cotton. And they'd hitch up the horses to what they called the go-down, it's a little old thing that you sat on and it had a blade stickin out each side that cut the weeds. And I'd go up and down the rows doin that. My mother always did outside work, the chores, milked the cows, raised turkeys, chickens, a garden. But it was all dry land farmin, never heard of irrigation till I don't know when—it just *wasn't*. And maybe you'd have a good crop, and maybe you *wouldn't*. If you didn't, you just moved on to another place. Course, that's why we moved so much!

Now my grandparents both had farms that they owned. But we were rentin. My mother is from a family of fifteen children. You ought

to hear her tell about all these deals, cause they worked in the fields just like a bunch of . . . well, I'll say "men." They did back then. They went to school very little. So did my father, went to school very little.

When I was a month old, my daddy had this string of horses. He traded horses even then. They had this covered wagon—I've got a picture of it—and they went from Oklahoma all the way to Kansas, trading horses on the way. While we were in Kansas, this covered wagon caught on fire. Mama was a-cookin fer a bunch of men and she rolled me up in a feather tick and threw me out! It's the truth! See, the stove exploded, and all she could think was to wrap me in the feather tick and throw me out through the fire. And see, my sister got out of it; but they didn't save a thing, save me and that feather tick! It was somethin to put it out, and there was no one there but her and my sister and myself. And I couldn't have been more than six months old. Everything they had was in that wagon!

I can remember my daddy a-tradin horses, I guess he was a horse trader all his life. He always liked 'em and knew 'em; this boy of ours, Clint Larry, he kind of takes after Daddy that way. Back then, you could make a good livin a-doin it. You'd be in one town and trade for a dozen horses, then you'd be in the next town and you'd sell 'em or trade 'em off. And well, it wouldn't be more than two or three dollars back then, but that came to good money. And then he did the cattle too; anywhere you'll go around here now they'll talk about how good a cattle buyer he was. He was always *fair* about it.

My daddy was a heavy-set man, not much taller than Clintie, and he had a way with him, everbody seemed to get along with him. I was never much good at judging cattle, but he could. He could jest look at 'em and figure out what they'd bring.

Woodward, Oklahoma, that was the town where he had this string of horses, and he did the road work. And we lived in a tent. A great big old long tent. One time, they sent Oveda and me home from school, we was sick. Let's see, what did we have that time? We must have had the measles. Cause here we are, jest as sick as we can be, and they had one of them Oklahoma windstorms and that dadgome tent blowed down on us! And Mama had to go out and get the men to come and put the tent back up!

This was before the Dust Bowl was the worst, cause then we were livin in Bealle. We lived out in the country then and you know it got so bad that whenever . . . well, they'd turn school out, and durin the day, it would be just as dark as night. They would turn on the streetlights, and the ones that did have cars drove with their lights on. It was that bad, we'd hang wet sheets up to the doors and windows and keep a changin them. I can remember that real easy.

When we lived in the tent, my mama was cookin for the bunch that worked for Daddy on the road. They all lived in little tents, and we had this long tent. We slept at one end, and Mama and Daddy and usually one of her sisters was with us. I had one aunt named Alvaretta that was with us; and another one named Gladys—she was at that time a widda, really she was divorced—and she had a little girl. And we just usually had a *good* time. Mama worked awful hard, though, she always worked awful hard, my mama did. She was cookin fer ten or twelve men probably, no runnin water, no nothin. Wood stove. My sister and I helped when she could get us to!

But we left Oklahoma in 1936. The first time we left, I remember goin to Little Rock, Arkansas. And what we did, we rented I guess a semitruck, and we put the household furniture, what we had of it, up front. And then Daddy loaded up these horses, he couldn't give up these horses! We went to Little Rock, Arkansas, and hoped to find a place down there. I was about ten. We got there right in the middle of the summer when it couldn't have got any hotter, and none of us lasted. So we loaded up agin and come right on back!

I'm tryin to remember, my mama and daddy also decided to move to California one time. They must have had a Model A. We went out there and stayed in Orange, California. I was real little then. And I don't know, I must've always been about to get burned up, cause I backed up to whatever kind of stove they had out there then, and caught my dress tail on fire. And I run out the door, and they had to throw me down and put it out. And comin back, when they crossed whatever the hottest part is, the car broke down, and I can remember us bein stranded out there in that desert. But we were on a bridge and I know we just moved in under that dadgome bridge! Daddy went on to the town to get somebody to help with the car and Mama got us settled under the bridge. I don't know how long we were there, I know we were little and we got awful restless. Seems like everywhere we went, we were always havin troubles! Times were hard, and the cars . . . we *thought* we always had good cars!

You know, my mama has always been restless. Still is. Right now, she's tryin to dream up movin somewhere! See, my daddy died whenever I was nineteen, so she's been a widda all these years. She's restless, she goes from one town to another, but she always does end up comin back to T or C [Truth or Consequences, New Mexico].

Then another time, we were back in Woodward, Oklahoma, *that* was the time I graduated from the eighth grade, and that time my daddy got to dealin more in the cattle. He went out to all these places and did the buyin. Since I didn't have any brothers, he always let me go with him. I was always used to goin with him, and he let me *drive.* My sister stayed with my mama and I got to go with my daddy. I was just my daddy's boy, I'd guess you'd say. I went out with him because it interested me. I've always been, as you can tell, interested in talkin! An when you go around and buy cattle, naturally you see the different ranches and meet the people at all the places.

And I guess that's why I go with Clintie so much, is because you know, I always thought that was the thing to do, cause that's what I grew up doin. Daddy'd let me do the figures, whenever you'd buy these cattle and you'd weigh them, why he'd let me do the figures. And he'd let me help weigh 'em. So Clintie, he does the same thing, he lets me do all the figurin and keepin the books. That's what I did for my daddy and I just kept a-doin it. Once in a while, Clintie wonders where the money went to, and I have to get out the checkbook and decide!

But my mother—you know I said she was the one you should talk to—we lived at this one place and it was called Nine Mile Creek and she went out to get some wood, and Daddy was off tradin some horses. It was very, very cold and she got in the quicksand. She thought that creek was froze enough that she could walk across it, to get this wood which looked better to her on the other side. And whenever she came back across, why she just went down! She clawed and she clawed that bank until she finally got herself out. But whenever she got to the house —she had left my sister and I in the house, and I don't imagine I was more than five years old and my sister would be six—Mama was just muddy from her chest down and just icy cold. She says she was "like to dyin and goin." She knew that quicksand was there, but she just thought it was frozen, and it wasn't.

Oh she's had lots of deals happen to her like near-accidents. And she always was restless. Fact is, most of the moves were her idea; she was always wonderin if it wouldn't be better in another town, or ready to move to a different place just to see what it was like. And after my daddy died, she sold the house in El Paso. And since then, she's just been from one town to another. She's just made her way all these years. That is thirty-five years, he's been dead that long. She worked the harvest, like if she was in California or Phoenix. She has sisters in Phoenix and they all work the fields, trim lettuce, and do the oranges, the cantaloupes . . . whatever you call that kind of work. And motel work . . . I think thirteen different years she went to Reno and did motel work just for the season, then she's ready to go on to somewhere else. She writes to people all over the area, and they do to her. She's livin in T or C. But right now she's tryin to figure out how to get to Reno and do a little more gamblin! She's seventy-eight. And she would just love to go to Reno again and play the slot machines, but it's kind of hard for her to find work at her age!

I met Clintie when I was fifteen. Well, the first time I ever *went* with him, I was fifteen. But he's six years older than I am. I'd be here in Corona for six months, my daddy'd be buyin cattle here in the fall; then by the second semester, we had moved to El Paso and Daddy bought cattle out of old Mexico. My sophomore and junior years, I went half of it up here and half down there. And my senior year, I went the whole of it in El Paso. By that time, my daddy'd had a stroke and that was whenever he quit buyin cattle.

And I would come up here, my mother and I would come up here to see to this little place that we had north of Corona, we had a ranch. It was about six sections [thirty-six hundred acres] and at one time we had angory goats and then we had cattle.

And then I guess how I got with Clintie, well, my daddy liked him. And naturally, I did too! But anyway, Mama and me would come back up here and see to the ranch. And Clintie would go out there with us and help us. And he helped round up this big bunch of horses whenever we sold them. And helped us work the cattle, deliver the calves. Oh, if there was anything to be done, I was out there doin! The brandin, or the what . . . I remember one time we went out to brand the colts and it was quite an experience. And anyway, my daddy gave me one. There really wasn't too many people had that big a bunch of horses—oh, you might have had six or eight—but he had about seventy-five head of mares, and you know that was somethin! But my daddy let me have this one colt, if I could break it. And I thought that would be pretty easy but you know it *wasn't!* You get a little old colt on the end of a rope and it's not funny at all whenever you don't know what to do! And I didn't! It just wasn't what I thought it was gonna be. But I did get that colt gentled down.

Even back in Oklahoma, as I say, we always had the horses. And if we had any little colts, well, I always claimed 'em. And I know one time my sister and I went down in the corral and she helped me up on this one colt; it was gentle enough that you could get up to it. And she helped me up on it. Well, it immediately pitched me off again! And they got after us good, wanted to know why we did it. And I said, "Well, that just looked so soft, and I just wanted to know what it would do!" But we didn't do that any no more, either!

So I got married when I was eighteen. Clintie always says he had to wait for me to grow up! Really we never did go together too much, because of the distance. But I did write him letters all the time. He wrote me about once a week, and I wrote him 'bout ever day! But see, he didn't have no telephone, so we couldn't call each other. Oh, we were very interested, both of us, but the distance was far, far for us. I guess I had come up here to see about Daddy's place and we talked about it, and then I had a letter from him afterwards saying that as soon as they got done taggin the sheep, then he would come to El Paso and we could get married. And this was very exciting—you don't do it too often!

And at that time, people didn't have these big weddings like they do now. And in El Paso you had to wait three days. So he came down on the train and we went to town the next day and bought the rings. And he asked my daddy—*after* we had bought the rings. Oh, Daddy knew what was goin on, from me, but Clintie actually *asked* him! So we got ready and went up to Las Cruces and got married, cause in New Mexico you didn't have to wait three days. Clintie couldn't be gone that long, he didn't *think!*

His father is very, very nice, very—oh!—mannerly. I often wondered what he thought about us! We lived with them four months while they were havin this house built for us. I imagine it was quite an adjustment for them to have had just three boys and then to have me move in with them! At that time, in nineteen forty-two, Clintie was workin for his dad, and gettin thirty dollars a month. When we got married, he started gettin forty-five dollars a month, so I guess you could say I was worth fifteen dollars!

I was married exactly a year when my daddy died. And then the year that he died, that was the year that I had JoEtta. She was born the next December. I had the three children in less than three years. Two years and nine months, to be exact. There's a year and ten days between JoEtta and Clint Larry. And then between Clint Larry and Lon, there's a year and nine months. You want to hear what names I dreamed up for them things? Let's see, LaVeda JoEtta is the girl, and then the first boy is Clint Larry, and the youngest is Lonnie Frank, and then you add Sultemeier onto that!

When we got married we didn't have no overhead water tank, so whenever the windmill turned, why we just went down and got a bucket of water. And then we carried it up to the house. The first overhead tank we had, we ordered this cedar storage tank out of Montgomery Ward. And we built that platform and put it up there, and it made the water flow. Well, we thought that was about the snazziest thing anybody had! I didn't have runnin water when I had JoEtta. I don't believe we got it in but about a month before I had Clint Larry.

When I had JoEtta, they decided—like all these women and older people do, that this one should do *that* and that one should do *this*—so they decided that I should move to town. "They" would be Clintie, Mrs. Sultemeier, my mother, Clintie's brother Frankie and his wife Jean! So we rented us an apartment in Corona. Really, you didn't go to the doctor every month, with *this* doctor. You went maybe two or three times. But because of it bein in the wintertime, and the snowstorms in this area, well, we rented an apartment and my mother came up to stay with me. Clintie stayed in town a good bit too—he would come back out to the ranch during the day and come into town when he could at night. Until I'm sure he gived his self out, running back and forth! The night she was born, about nine o'clock Clintie went up and got this Dr. Berry and it was snowing, so he told us to come up and spend the night in his house. So we went up there about twelve and she was born about five, I believe.

But this Mexican woman Dr. Berry had workin for him, her name was Maggie Meyers. And there I was about to have a baby, and the first thing I knew there she was in the kitchen a makin a batch of cookies! But whenever I had JoEtta, Dr. Berry had this room in the back of the house, and I know this sounds odd, but Clintie stayed right there with me. He was right there when all three of ours was born, and he helped tend to the babies. But not too many did that then, but that was the way ours was did. All I ever had was a little bit of chloroform right at the last, so I was out when I had all three. Nowadays, they do this modern stuff, but I always had some and was out. So really Clintie knows more bout all that than I do. If you need any help a-havin one, he'd be the one to ask!

And whenever Clint Larry was born then, which was just a year later, whenever I decided that I might be pregnant then, I wouldn't tell anybody when it—well, I never did really know too close on that myself—and I told 'em "Oh, I thought maybe February." But it didn't work out that way.

The thing is, you didn't particularly *talk* this free about bein pregnant. Probably nobody didn't realize it until up in the summer, that I *was* pregnant. You just didn't talk about it. Back then, you didn't go at a month or two months to the doctor. You just realized what you realized, and you kept it to yourself! Well, now, Clintie knew. We've always talked very—now you know some women might not talk to their husbands about somethin like this—but he knows everthing I ever thought or *did! Very much so!* And when I realized it—well, I had tried to nurse JoEtta, I *did* nurse her for three months, and you weren't supposed to get pregnant when you were nursin! So I never did really know the date. So I said February, but he come in December. But I think, really, that it was that I was just a little bit embarrassed, so I just said the first thing that come to me, and then I let it be!

But I was nursin JoEtta for three months and really I shouldn't have, cause I didn't have enough milk. But I didn't know any better, and consequently we had a baby that cried all through the night. Now Clintie's favorite deal is tellin all these people how we had this basket on rollers and he spent all that time a shakin that basket till he could shake it in his sleep! So he shook the baby all night and I walked the floor with her durin the day!

Now whenever we came and figured out where we were gonna put this house, Clintie's daddy stood right here and said, "What you want to do is put it where you can see the falls when the Gallo runs."

That arroyo there is a dry canyon and it's called the Gallo and it starts up at Corona and runs clear through here and eventually into a canyon called the Macho. But it's a long, long deal, and some places there are these high bluffs. And if they have a two-inch rain up above, it really gets big. And it is, it's just like livin in a different country when it runs, it just *rolls* off that falls and there's a swimmin hole up there. And all of the kids have to come, that's what they want to do is go play in the Gallo. And that Gallo has run around this house. And if it comes down, you don't have to worry about anybody comin to visit, cause they can't get across! And we're just here! Oh, it's pretty, it surely is. There's somethin about it—like I said, we just couldn't change our minds to move across the canyon. We're the only ones that have that problem, I guess, that can't get in or out their house! But that Gallo's real fascinatin that it'll run so big and so fast.

When you go into Corona for the mail, which you have to do, that's forty miles in and out. You know sometimes now, it seems as cheap to call somebody. If I didn't have a reason to go to town, I could call cheaper than I could go to town to mail the letter!

We got the phone out there about twenty-two years ago. We built it ourselves. There's about eighteen ranchers from Corona on down, and everbody in that bunch put in so much money and everbody worked on it. It made a big difference. Before, a lot of us felt more isolated. And now you can go talk to somebody for ten or fifteen minutes —course, the men all say we talk for an hour!

But I don't believe I felt *real* isolated before. It's like people say, "Well, aren't you bored, or feelin isolated, or whatever?"

But you *never* know, when you get up, what kind of a day you're goin to have! Now just like today, look what happened: here the gates are all knocked down by some drunk plowin through 'em, and here's this woman come from California to visit! Well tomorrow, it may be no tellin what! And you really never know from one day to the next what you could do.

Now, my sister has her life planned out for a year ahead what she's goin to do! And it'll pretty well sit that way. Now, I could *not* make plans, that it would ever actually happen that way! Like if anybody asks us to do anything this time of year, we'll say, "Oh, we can't, we're gonna shear!"

Now that shearin just takes one day, but we'll take on about it for a month. It'll take that long to get it did. Actually it's jest a one-day affair, but the way we all act . . . well now, it'll take several days to drive the stock in. And we don't know exactly when the shearin crew is a-comin. A good shearin crew can do a thousand, twelve hundred head in a day. I've did the drivin on a horseback and I've did it in a pickup. Now that we're a little more modern, I will take the pickup and when we get them all rounded, I can bring them in from that Irvine ranch to this ranch without a horse. But Clintie still prefers to drive with the horseback, even if his brothers do use the motorcycles!

Then there's always these accidents. I think the worst one we ever had was, we were roundin up to deliver lambs to the market, which would be in October, and I was a-ridin that day, and Clint Larry and Clintie. And there weren't very many in the pasture, but we were tryin to get the ones we hadn't gotten with the big bunch. We was all kind of split up and Clintie come to me and says that Clint Larry's horse had stepped in a gopher hole and fell with him, and broke Clint Larry's arm. Well that dadgome horse was the gentlest one we ever had, it was the one JoEtta grew up a-ridin! Shows, you can't tell . . . they'll say "Oh, the horse is gentle," well, you can't never tell . . . an this one broke Clint Larry's arm, both bones. And this happened whenever he was sixteen years old. Well, here we are up in the roughest pasture we got. Clintie come and got me, and he turned my horse and Clint Larry's loose and left me there with Clint Larry. Then he rode back in and got the jeep. And he come back up there, no road, no nothin. And we got Clint Larry in that jeep with the saddle blanket to kinda keep that arm from jarrin, probably the worst thing we coulda did. Cause of all the dirt in the blanket, and see, it was both bones stickin out. So whenever we got to the house and called the doctor, he said well, he'd be waitin for us when we got to Roswell. And that's ninety-one more miles, and the road wasn't paved then! It's thirty-five miles to the main road, and that thirty-five miles is pretty bad. Oh I did real good until it was all over with, then I didn't do too good, you know!

An then two years ago, Clint Larry's wife, Lee, broke her leg right in the middle of deliverin. Her horse hit a cactus and pitched her off, an broke her leg. As I say, you *never* know from one day to the next what's gonna happen . . . but like for it to be *that* kind of thing, you don't expect it!

We think that what makes good sheep herders is starting them young. Girls and boys, the whole bunch. I can show you pictures of mine, I guess I was out there with 'em when they was just babies! Nowadays, when these kids are fourteen, sixteen years old they think they know more than their parents . . . where in our day, clear till mine were out of high school and even in college, well in those days we just had one car and, well, we all went *together* or we just didn't go! An when we stayed here, we all worked together too.

Now we do still all visit together, all the Sultemeiers, this *clan,* or bunch . . . whenever we shear, as I told you, we get ready for it for a month. All right now, already JoEtta has givin the orders, she and her bunch want to come down. And I've got a picture last year when we sheared, there was twenty-four kids here. And they'd all get down there and play in them wool sacks!

Clintie's got a lot of relatives. You have no idea how many relatives! When I first married that was one of the things they all told me, "You don't want to talk about anybody because they may be a kin to you!" You see, I had no relatives at all. I had my mother over at T or C, and all my relatives are either California, Arizona, or there's a few back in Oklahoma there. I maybe have more than Clintie does, but his have mostly stayed right here. I think that's a real nice thing. Now you may not be kin to one person, but you may have some relatives in common. Now there's one person that I feel close to, and let's see, her husband and my husband, they have the same aunts and uncles. So if you know that they're relatives, you just have a little closer feelin to them.

I never have been around JoEtta since she got married as much as Mrs. Sultemeier was with me. But if I'm around her, I'm a-givin advice, sames as the older ones did to me. We have quite a few young families around here, and actually the ones that their parents are not here, the girls will call me and ask me questions. They don't none of them seem to resent me giving my advice. They just most of them have young children, about like Clint Larry's, and they just call and ask, tell me this or that, and I've always got an answer, right or wrong. The young girls, they like to call me Granny, and I say, "All right! Granny here knows!" After all, I *do* have eight grandchildren!

Clintie says I'm always wantin to know *why*. I'm always askin why, and never gettin nothin did! But he always does answer! Well, there has to be a reason to me; why either there's a reason, or you wouldn't do it. And it's hard to get them to explain that reason sometimes! But if I can't figure out why, I ain't about to do it!

I'm still in love with my husband. I get mad at him sometimes, but we're still very much in love. I guess you might say, we jest have a good time here. We always did, and we still do!

III

WORK

We're a Different Kind
of Couple
Gladys Sampson

The Sampson farm, as you drive up to it, is an archetypical midwestern farm. The two-story clapboard farmhouse sits on a slight rise looking benevolently down on fertile fields of corn and soybeans. The large yard is tree-shaded and carefully mowed. All around is a feeling of quiet prosperity.

Gladys Sampson has lived on that farm for all of her eighty-one years. Since before her husband's death, she has farmed it in partnership with her son, Gerald. Even now, her regular jobs include discing the farm's 180 acres of crop lands (breaking up plowed land with a tractor and disc harrow) and using her smaller tractor to keep the several acres of lawn mowed.

My grandfather bought this land and moved here with his family, when my dad was about seven years old. My dad got married and started out right here too. His father was living till two years after I was born, so I suppose they just went on working together. Then when I was twelve, the old house was moved down into what was the orchard, and this house was built here.

At the time I was growing up, it was all horses, wind power. We didn't have tractors till the boys come along. Nineteen thirty-six was when we got our first tractor. There were two orchards here when I was a girl. We had every type of apple then, it seemed like. Cherry trees all the way from here to the barn. Cows, chickens, and horses. The barn would be full of horses and mules, work horses and road horses. There weren't any cars or anything at that time, you know. I could ride horseback up to the country school and just hang the reins over her neck and she'd come right home.

Well I grew up right out here, around the farm all the time. My father'd give me that finger and I'd hang on and go with him. He had me around a lot. He and I got along fine. I've said that I only remember one spanking, and Mother gave me that. And I always said I didn't deserve that, cause what I was accused of, I hadn't done. But Dad and I always got along beautifully. He liked to have me *with,* and I just wanted to be *with.* So I trailed around out here, when they were feeding cattle and it was all muddy. Well, I guess that was after my boys got big, too. But when I was little I used to go and break the ears of corn with Dad, we didn't have shelled corn like we do now, so I'd help him break the ears. And I always had ponies. I just liked the outdoors, I always did. Mother said I should have been a boy instead of a girl!

I got married in January of nineteen twenty. The folks were married in eighteen ninety-seven on January twenty-first, and I was married on January twenty-first, nineteen twenty. My aunt, my mother's sister, married five years before Mother on that same day. Levi was living just a mile straight south of here, you can still see the buildings where his folks lived. I don't know how I met him. But he was in the World War I in the meantime, before we were married. I had my ring before he went in service. Lots of them got married first but I . . . we didn't prefer it that way. We lived with my folks for over a year, I guess, and then they moved to town. And then my father started farming down on the other side of town. Dad never did really retire, except the very last years it got so he pretty much had to. He farmed a place north of here too. But I was an only child and they always insisted that I live here. So that's how come they moved off and let me stay on.

After I got married I helped with all kinds of farm work: I loaded hay, I fed the horses, and curried horses, I milked, I taught both boys how to milk. I sowed oats, walking back of the feeder. And I dragged, walking back of a drag. I picked corn all fall side by side with my husband. I disced all the fields so Gerald could plant this year. But that's a tractor that has a cab, that's like sittin in the house! Air conditioning, heater, music. Quite a difference from walking behind the horses!

Levi and I were farming a hundred and sixty acres. Then, we had oats, corn, hay, and pasture for the animals. After I was married, I'd get up in the morning about four-thirty and make the bread, do the churning, hang our milk and cream in the well to get it cool, get that work done before breakfast. When I was growing up, they always said I could go out at nights if I'd be up in the morning. But back then I didn't have to be up till six o'clock. No, I wasn't overworked as a child. I worked more after I got married. For housekeeping we didn't have machines, you know.

I know I had as many as three hired men to feed, too. When Lowell was a baby he had the colic. I know I had to stand with one foot wheeling the crib while I did my other work. I wore the rubber right off the crib wheels! Now Gerald was so good I never wore out *that* set at all! But Lowell had this colic, and cried, and cried. I baked all the bread, canned all our meat, I don't know how to explain all that work to you now. When we butchered, I canned the meat, or fried it down, or smoked it. Made sausage. Had to have your own meat then, you couldn't just go to town all the time.

My first son, Lowell, was born here in the bedroom in nineteen twenty-two. But when Gerald was born in nineteen twenty-five, I went into the hospital in Waterman. You didn't go to the hospital just to have a baby those days. But I preferred to go to the hospital because I was running the whole place from the bed in there when Lowell was born. I couldn't sleep until everybody else was asleep. And of course, when the baby was born, we were haying. Levi got his finger caught in the pulley that took the hay up. And Mother had to come because I had bread sponge rising and she had to finish the bread. We'd been canning cherries. Let's see, I finished canning one hundred and six quarts the night before Lowell was born. Course, you canned everything then, you didn't go out and buy anything. Then the next day while the baby was coming, my husband got his finger caught in the pulley, it took off the end, some way. And of course, everybody was nervous. The baby didn't come till midday dinner and the crib wasn't together yet. And my mother was upset because the crib wasn't ready!

But the nurse, Mrs. Hadwell, who came, she wasn't concerned about what happened to anybody but her patient. So I had good care. But when Gerald came, well the doctor came and picked me up and took me to the hospital, because Levi stayed home with Lowell.

I think you have to spend a lot of time with a child, like they say, a lot of love. We didn't have this tube to entertain us. We'd read . . . and I taught them to do the milking and all that. Levi didn't do those things. Course, when it come time to teach field work, well that was his end of the deal. But I was outside so much. We had so much garden, you know, and the kids'd work along with me. They didn't have ever-thing to do with, like the kids now. Now, anything they see, they want. You see them in the stores, they're squealing, hollering for stuff. Well, we didn't get to the stores much; they didn't have those opportunities. They'd get one nice little toy and that'd do for a long time. I grew up cutting out pictures out of magazines, I've got some in a trunk in the attic yet that I thought were especially nice. And of course, I had no brothers or sister, so I had to learn to entertain myself. I never cared to play house much. It was ponies, dogs. Course, I had this horse that un-derstood me just like a person, did whatever I wanted.

The boys and I, we did all kinds of things with animals. We raised pet lambs, and we had pet pigs. One of the boys had a turkey that was quite tame. And we had a horse, a colt that needed to be bottle-fed several times a day, lots of things like that. You just took it as part of life that you had to raise the ones with no mothers like that.

Lowell, the older boy, influenced Levi pretty much to get a trac-tor. Levi hated to increase in new types of things. He thought it was the way to the poorhouse, burning up gasoline in cars and tractors! He never was very mechanically inclined. And then his father too . . .

well, they had five kids and they'd come through the Depression and it wasn't the go-ahead days *then* like it is now. My other son says now that it's a two-way standard the way we live here. Well, it's like with the old wood cookstove, I'd hate to do without it. We don't modernize anything in the house here. When I go, the next one won't like what I want, but it suits me.

In some ways, progress has made life much easier. But I don't know where I'd think it was as interesting. I'd think it was more boring to do one thing all day, make one little part for a machine. It was like when I was a girl, I worked down in the bank down here for a while and I learned how to do everything. Now, one person sits at a machine and just does that, where I had the fun of doing a little of everything. I can remember once we went through the packinghouse in Chicago and the women were packing dried beef all day long! I couldn't stand it. Out here on the farm, we did whatever was needed. You had to do everything for yourself, all kinds of things.

Well, it's changing constantly . . . I don't know whether it's for the better . . . it does give everybody things that they're entitled to, like a vacation, for instance. We did a *lot* of hard labor, putting up the crops, husking corn by hand, and all that, you know. It was pretty tiring and we had to work long days to get it accomplished. And it's different to go to town and buy your butter and all of that, than to milk the cows, and separate the milk, keep it cool, churn it, and work it: that was a lot of hard work to get a little butter. Some kids nowadays have *no* idea where food comes from, they just think it comes from the store!

Well, you can go through a lot of hardship that you wouldn't want to go back and go through again. And a lot of problems that you can solve if you have to. A lot of people now think for sure they couldn't go through some of the things we did. And yet if it come right down to it, they could do just as well, some of them better. When hard times come, you have to. But I don't know . . . people didn't live as long back then. Forty some years old, my grandmother was when she died.

Since I had my cataract eyes operated on, why, I haven't been up to par. Tractor work's not difficult. That's *much* better than housework, doesn't take as much energy. And I've got the field to myself as a rule. I feel *better* outside, I always did. I never liked housework. No, I didn't like it. My mother was a very persnickety one, I'd say, about her housework. Poor soul, she'd turn over if she could see what her house looks like here!

Gerald and I have just been together all the time. The last four or five years before he died, Levi wasn't feelin too good, so I worked out with Gerald all the time. And he has never . . . *well,* I know I would like to have roller-skated, and he says that he never wanted to teach me because he didn't want to be skating with his mother! But other than that, he never has hesitated about taking me to anything, where sometimes you'd think they might be ashamed to take their mother. We're not the usual couple, but we have traveled all over together, and have gotten along so well together!

Gerald did the plowing last fall. I did almost all of the discing this spring. Boy, that was a rough ride this year! You know we didn't have freezing and heaving because of all that snow. We've never before had it completely covered with snow for the whole winter, like this year, so it didn't get softened up. Ordinarily, fall plowing gets mellow after it's laid all winter. And I laid on this elbow awhile and then on that one awhile to save my seat! He was putting in corn. I disced nearly all the fall plowing, and then I disced all of it again before the planter. But he did do a little bit the first time. And then he disced around the fence because I couldn't be sure to see that good. And then, he took care of the greasing and fueling and all of that. I don't do anything but get in and drive it. I could fuel before this year, if I had the time. But ordinarily, he'd get that done while I'm still busy in the house here.

There's a lady across the road here that does everything now. I just disc, but she plows, she runs the combine, she . . . well, they've got new types of machinery now that we don't even have. Course, she doesn't have the work with livestock that I had. And then the lady neighbor over here still has the smaller machinery. And when I work on one side of the fence and she works on the other, well, really I feel sorry for her. We've tried to keep up with the modern somewhat; it's getting ahead of Gerald now, but he's getting to the age when things aren't so certain how long I'll be able to help. We've a different situation than a young married couple. A married couple, they're about the same age. And there's quite an age difference between us, nearly thirty years. Oh, and the next neighbor down here, she does everything too, she plows and combines and does everything. So I've got lots of company!

My mother lived to be ninety-three and a half, and my father was eighty-four. The doctor thinks my being so active is the best thing for me. I told him my other son doesn't agree with me being out in the fields so much, and he said, "Well if you can't set him straight, have him call me, I'll tell him."

I tell you, I've had one good heart attack. The other wasn't so much. But back in nineteen sixty-eight, I had a good one, and it was from high cholesterol. Well, I've had some troubles, but they go by. You forget some of them. Now since I've had my hip replacement, I haven't had a bit of pain in that hip. I was getting so I was in need of two canes some of the time. That's a wonderful operation for anyone that needs it. I recommend the hip replacement; I don't recommend the cataracts, however. That's been a disappointment. This eye is just like there's a big blob of water or something on that, it's all blurry. The other one is pretty clear, but it's dark. I guess I've been disappointed, or disillusioned, or whatever. You can get along half blind pretty well in your own home, but when you get out where it's all up and down, well that makes a big difference!

I haven't got much ambition left. It's so windy, I don't like to go out in all this wind. Now last night, the wind died down after blowin all day, so then I got the tractor out and did some mowing.

But since I've had my eye operations, I've felt old. Before that, I didn't realize the change. But I've had to—well, both eyes, you know— I've had to just sit. You can't lift, you can't lean over. And I began to get depressed, and I think you lose fast then. Now, I've accepted the fact that I'm going to have to live with it, that I'm not coming back like I used to.

When you get in your eighties, you begin to *sound* old, which I didn't used to. Well, Mother lived to be ninety-three and a half, so I didn't think much about it. But . . . well, I didn't realize or feel much difference. And even *yet* sometimes, I don't. But I just find out that I can't stand some of the work now. Jerry says he's aged more than I have. Maybe it's living with one older. And I've lived with him young and trying to keep up with him too. As I get older and lay around, he does too. I don't know, I can't figure out too much for myself, only that

I'm slowin down. If I work a couple hours—well, now, I did all the discing with the tractor and that doesn't bother me much—but if I clean two rugs, that's about that. Instead, I used to clean all four of them at once. So that's why I say that a year from September might be too late for me to see this book.

Well, on the tractor, you just sit there. And outdoors, as soon as I go outdoors I feel better. I never did get along inside very well; I've always liked to be outdoors. And you see, I have to go down on my knees to clean the rugs because I can't see it standing up. And ironing is the other thing that bothers me a good deal. I'm not as steady now, I hang on to things. Well, mostly because I can't see, I guess. When I go up and down steps now, I hang on to the railing. I'm just not as stable as I used to be. When I was younger, I never thought about getting old. It's just like now, in the morning when I wake up, I'm the same person I used to be, I think of things to do just like I did before. But I never accomplish it now . . . What is it they say, "Old soldiers don't die, they just fade away"? I guess that's just about how it is with me.

I Done Worked!

Lottie Jackson

Lottie Jackson has worked for almost forty years as a field hand on a three-thousand-acre farm in southwestern Georgia. She's believed to be in her seventies, possibly even older, but her birth date is unknown. Lottie is a worker, who takes great pride in her capacity to still put in an eight-hour day in the fields.

When I visited, the farm had recently been sold to a corporation of foreign investors. Lottie, like her friend Irene Nixon, was about to move away from the house where she had expected to finish out her life. At the time of this interview, that was her most pressing concern.

I been out all day planting watermelon vines. Lord, if I didn' work I couldn't make it. No, if I didn' work, I'd jus die! I been workin ever day, *ever* day, in those big fields by myself. I *like* to work. I jus *want* to work, cause that keep me goin. I be jus settin round, I get so *stiff*, you know. I walked through the fields, worked out there every day, workin for Mr. John, you know. Yes suh, I been here ever since forty, right here on this place. Been here ever since forty! Been a *long* time. Came here young and done got old.

An I tole Mr. John, he better *not* throw me away! I done *raised* his chillun that's got grown and gone away. I said, "Now you better see bout me!"

An he say, "Lottie, I'm gonna see bout ya."

I said, "I knowed it cause if you don', I'm a-comin to your house! You ain't gettin rid of Lottie!"

An he jus laughed. "Lottie, we ain't gonna throw you away."

"You better not, cause I'm almos one of the family, I'm one *in* the family!" That what I tell him.

I hate movin so *bad!* But he say, "Lottie, I cain't help it, I had to do it."

It got confused in the famly some way. I tole him he ought've looked out for us, though, he ought've leaved a space for us. I ain't goin to no town, not Dawson an not Americus, neither! An I cain't find me no house, cause they ain't no houses, ain't no house cause people is tearin 'em down soon's as people move out. I got to try to get me a trailer house or somethin. Somethin to live in. There ain't no houses.

Lord, I don' like no town, for sure I don'! I like to stay out where I can get *somptin* fer nothin! I kin go to somebody's house they give me some greens, peas, anything. If I go to town, I got to go to the market. Town ain't no place to live!

I fish a lot, I sure do. How come I goin to miss this place, we got a lot of fishin on this place. An I hate to leave here, on account of that fishin. I like to fish! There's a heap of dams down there where the beavers done dammed and jus left a little stream, made ponds out of it.

I go from one pond to another, I catch 'em, I sure do! Trout, bass, catfish, all kinds!

Oooh, I had one of the purrrtiest gardens. But I don' have one now. See, I didn't know where I was gonna be. See, I'd've had this place cleaned up all the way around, but I let it growed up cause I didn' know *where* I was gonna be. My garden, I jus let it growed up. I grow beans, greens, peas, everthing like that. Oh, I have plenty of flowers in my yard, all kind of flowers in my yard.

Irene older than I am, I know that. I was born in Calhoun County but I don't know when I was born. Don't even know my mama because she died in chil'bed. Didn't never even see my mama. I had one brother, he die when I be a little thing like that; an one sister, she died year before last. Ain't nobody left but me. My aunt, one of my aunts, raised me. Didn't know my dad till I was bout grown! Sure didn't. Sure *didn't!*

Our aunt raised us. Not my brother, he died when us wasn't but little things. He was older than us. He had a *heap* of sense, you know. An he went over to fix the cane mill, they had a cane mill what had stopped, you know; and it caught him and it broke his neck.

My aunt had some more chilrun, you know, what their parents had died and she was raisin them with us. She didn't have none of her own. She had a husband that died; she were a widda. Her good. She was *good* to us. She was on her own place, she had hands workin for her, an a big old stove. She took care of us good. Dad, he'd come for us, but she'd tell us that wadn't our daddy, you know. Us'd run from him, us'd *run* from him! She did that to keep our daddy from gittin us, you know, and us didn' know no better, us'd jus *run* from him.

When I were at my aunt's, I jes worked in the field. Worked in the fields! Didn't get time to go to school fer in the fields! Yeah'm that what I did, work in the fields or in da house. Weren't nothin to do in the fields, then I were in the house. You go on in there, an they put you to work. I growed up workin, growed *up* workin! Sure did.

No'm they never tell me how old I was. Wouldn't tell you cause they think that make you grown! No, they sure wouldn't. Didn't do nothin but work ye, sure would work ye now. I'm *glad* they did it. I'm glad of it. Sure 'nough. Made me willin to do it right on.

Now my sista, she wasn't much of a worker, an I'd work hard, you know. I work hard enough fer her, where her wouldn't get a whuppin! She was older than I was, an I'd work *hard*. I'd show up right smart, you know, to keep her from a-whuppin us. My sista cared that they whup her, but she jest a slow worker, couldn't work much. She scared of a whupping but she couldn't make work. I'd ruther be like I am.

Irene sure had a hard life. I didn't have it hard like she did. I have worked *hard,* but she have done some things *I* didn' do.

When I were a little girl, I were choppin cotton, pickin cotton, all of that. Tha's right. First of the year, start plowin, pickin them old stalks, pilin them up. You didn' have no time for sittin around! Sure didn'. Ooooh girl, you better get up afore the sun rise, better get on out there afore the sun be up, or she be there with a strap. Yes ma'am! You better get up. Yes ma'am, you *better* get out of that bed! I'd wake up and wake the others up. She'd fix a breakfast for us, and she'd have that breakfast ready where we could hit the field. Soon's we was done, we had to git on. Sure did! They jes tell me what they want done. I never was hard to learn nothin. They tell me or show me *one* time, that be it, I'd do it.

We didn' have no birthdays, none of that, just "Go to the field!"

No, we didn' know nothin bout birthdays! Christmas they bring us a
little Santa Claus at night, give you an apple or orange, little candy,
somptin like that. Bake a little cake, or somptin. Chillun gettin so
much now, they don' want *this* an they don' want *that,* they kin get
anything they want! Us was glad to git a biscuit on Sunday mornin!

An I done some of everthing in the field that could be done. I
done plowed. Me an my huband, we worked that farm up there, just
me an him. An I worked! I'd help him plow an he'd help me hoe. And
come time together, we'd get our supper ourself. An then get out and
help the other. Plowin with mules. We were sharecroppin. That where
my huband died, up there. I think my huband died in . . . fifty-two
. . . fifty-three! That right, he died in fifty-three. An I didn' have not
nair a chile, not nair a one. Sure didn't.

I left my aunt's house after I married. I don' know how old I was.
Round fifteen, sixteen year old, I think. I think I were that old cause
they wouldn't let you marry along then fore you got old enough, you
know. Chillun nowadays, they don' marry, they jus shack up together,
they don' marry no more! Now an then, you find one that will marry,
but mos they jest git together an say, "That my huband, that my wife."
But you had to *marry* along in then. I think it better to get married.

You ask what'd I *do* when I got married!? Worked a farm! I
moved to a place, jes me and my huband. An Lord, I jes work, work,
work, work. I work harder here though, than I did then. I done some
WORK on this place. An I wud be doin it now, if Mr. John be farmin
it still! I'd be in the fields right now, sure I would. All over this place,
I worked jus by myself. Nobody wif me. He'd come back and forth,
see if nothin got at me. I'd be workin way out back and he'd come
ever night an see if anything got me! He'd tell me what to do, but a

heap a time, I'd tell him. "This place need to be worked, Mr. John."

"Well, Lottie, go ahead and do it," he'd say.

I never drove no tractor, I wished I'd've but if I did, I wudn't know how to turn it around! I tole him, "Mr. John, jus learn me how to turn it around, I'll drive it!" But he never did learn me. I hated fer the mules to go. I hated that. I like mules. I wanted to go *fast*. I wanted a fast mule, I didn't want no mule draggin. I wanted one gotta *go* when I went.

An I liked to shake peanuts an pick cotton. I liked-ed that. I put peanuts up, fast as my huband could plow them up. He'd get mad an take out the mule an go to the house! He wanted me to be slow where he could help shake some. He mad, he *mad!* Sure was!

I love to cook. I likes to cook, if I gots somethin to cook, I likes to do it. My huband cooked when I be workin sometimes. When we got through with our farmin, he wouldn't want me to go out nowhere an work. But I'd go out anyhow, an he'd stay home, look out for the cows and cook! I'd work and he'd fuss . . . you know, I'd work my farm, then I'd go out an work, but he'd stay home and cook. He'd say when I done did my work, I ought to stay home an rest. But I'd go work an help other folks. Sometime he'd go, an most time he wudn't.

I worked, you *know* I worked. I'd plow an I'd plant. Get done plantin, it be hoein time. Yes sir, I done some work. And I still would be, followin them tractors, handin seed, *everthing.*

Them tractors put a lot of folks out of work. It were a bad time. Don't know what gonna happen to us now either, I jus don' know! Lately now, I been figurin maybe they fixin to put us in *slavery times* agin!

You cain't get this an you cain't get that. No work, an no houses, no gas, *nothin*. Food up yonder so high you cain't buy it. I jus don' know what gonna happen. Ever year but this, I growed my food, but this year everthing done turned around. I don' have a garden cause I didn' know where I was gonna be. I jus don' know what we goin to do! I ain't hear none of 'em talk bout slavery times lately, but I think on it.

It sure was worser in slavery times! In my times, we wudn't make much, but we'd get some, sure would! Maybe two hundred dollars fer the whole year. But fer us, that'd be—you know, when I first came here on this place, they weren't givin but fifty cent a day. An my huband were gittin sixty cent. He got sixty cause he was a man, I reckon, and I were a lady. An I worked harder than him, cause he couldn't work like me. That right! Sure did seem wrong to me, but I jus couldn't do no better. I hear some of 'em say they work for a quarter a day. I ain't never worked for no twenty-five cent a day, but I hear some of these folk round here say they *have* worked for twenty-five cents a day!

An I'm talkin bout you had to go to the field before sunup an work till the *bell* rang, an go back at one o'clock an work till *dark*. That right! For that money! Fifty cent! An come back an wash, an cook, an all that in the dark.

One time, my huband an me, we was with some white people wouldn't give us nothin. Was *worthless* folk, an wouldn't give us nothin. We couldn't hardly git somptin to eat. So we moved over here. We stayed at that other place two years. Sure did. Cause we couldn't git nothin, we moved over here. I had knowed bout this place fore we came here. When we was down at them white folks, we'd visit some people, that stayed over here. So that how we knowed bout this place an we moved on over here. Been here ever since. I stayed here till my huband died, and I'm *still* here. Done pretty good on this place.

My huband had cancer. He was sick about two year. Sure was. Ooooh Lord, like to have bout worked me to *death!* I had to see bout him, an work that crop, an I had two mules, and four or five head of cows to see bout. You know, people'd come over there an help me wid him; Irene an them, they help me wid him. I had to keep a fire goin, you know, all day long, an I jus bout cleaned up them woods up there cuttin wood! To keep him warm. When some of them be there wif him, I'd go cut wood.

An he'd tell me, "Honey, I ain't gonna hurt right now, you kin go ahead an do what you gotta do. I ain't gonna hurt right now."

So, I'd get out an go do, an run back. I'd work out in the field an jus run back see bout him, sure would! When he went down, I worked, sure 'nough, cause I had *all* it to do! The cows an the mules, an seein bout him. His name Richard Jackson, but everbody called him Shorty. He bout a high as Irene. But he weren't little, he were stout!

My life didn' change much after he were gone. I got on just bout as good as when he was livin.

I couldn't do without my huband, you know, cause he was *good* to me. But I wouldn't have nair an un now! Uh uh, I'm doin *too* good!

You know, the Lord is removing the men, cause they ain't no good.. More men die than the women, cause they ain't no good! Sure does! Why I coulda married the next week after my huband had died. The next *week,* they talkin bout marryin me! They knowed I was a hard worker an they thought I might take care of 'em! But I didn't want none of 'em! NOOOOOO! My huband been gone all that long, an I ain't married yet. An I'm doin all right. But my huband was good to me, sure was.

I never liked frolickin like Irene did. No, I *never* liked that. I always been *old,* all of my days! Yeah, my sista was fast, like Rene. She'd get mad, you know, if I wudn't go out with her.

She'd tell me, "You'm too *slow!*"

"Yeah, I aim to be here a *long* time slow!"

I took care of myself, sure did. After my huband died, my sista and her fella'd come here trying to take me out. But I wudn't come out the door. I wudn't run my life out, uh uh! Got to take *care* of myself! I ain't missed a thing, not nothin. My sista's dead and *gone* now an I'm still right here.

Irene, she still here, but she ain't no *good* fer anything. She *here* all right. She can do her work round the house an everthing, she might could do a little work in the field maybe, but it wouldn't be much. Rene want to do, and she sure got the will. She sure do got the *will.* She ain't lazed up a bit. But sometime she cain't, cause she be hurtin. I know she older than I am. An I is old, I'm pushin well on over seventy. I is *old.*

I seen some young people look older than I do! Young folk! Look older than I do! This day, OLD women look better than the chillun. Some of these old folk that got grown chillun look better than the chillun, that right! You know, I be *thankful* that I'm old an can be doin anything that I've been doin. I'm thankful! I do the *same* work I ever done. I thank the Lord for bein old an doin what I want to do!

Plenty old ones and plenty young ones cain't do nothin. Everthing I ever done, I still do now: cut wood, tote wood, work in the field, tote them big buckets ever day, time I put the buckets down, I got to hoe, hoe this big place, just me, that's right, fillin up them big tractors with peanuts an gettin them things. Big five-gallon buckets full of peanuts, one in each hand, and all them boys be turnin them big tractors, "All right, come on!" An I got to be right there with 'em.

I work ever day *now*. I work wif a man that go round an hire hands, you know. He hires hands an tell you what place to work. The man pay us eighteen dollar a day. Some works by the hour, different places, but he just pay so much a day. We go to the field at eight ever day and work till eleven, an then we go back at one-thirty an work till six after noon. Not bad pay, when I have worked for fifty cent a day!

But I cain't work much an get my Social Security. They don' like you to be workin. I kin make more money workin than I kin on Social Security. Sure! See, if I were on Social Security they don' pay but once a month an I can get money ever day workin!

Yeah, that Mr. John, he a good one. He look out for me. I said to his boy, I said to Mr. Dave, "If I get where I cain't do nothin, you better see bout me! I done set up wif you all day an all night when you was a little bitty thing, couldn't do nothin. An you better see bout me now!"

I bathed them chillun, bathed 'em an put 'em to bed! I set up there with 'em all night. Mr. John and them be gone, an I set up there *all* night till he come back, till *day* the next morning. An them chillun are bout grown now.

Yeah, the years don' stop now, they roll around. Sure do. One year roll round, an here come another one agin! An still here, thank the Lord! Yes sir, I been here with these people a *long* time!

That Old Ocean'll Get You
Jennie Cirone

Jennie Cirone lives in South Addison, on the northern coast of Maine. She lobster-fishes with her husband and her brother, and raises sheep on her own on two islands off the Maine coast.

The second time I visited, it was sheep-shearing day on Jennie's island. I joined a crew of neighbors and relatives, and Jennie's brother ferried us out to the island. Jennie greeted us at the shore, and her longtime friend Doris called to us from the cabin, "Homemade dough-nuts and fresh coffee!" The day passed in a happy, exhausted haze as I helped shear sheep to earn my keep, delighted in Doris's roast goose dinner, and enjoyed the companionship of Jennie's shearing crew.

She has gathered a large circle of young friends, nieces and nephews, local residents, and "out-of-staters" for miles around who are making a living from the land. As one of the shearers told me, "There's no one I'd rather go to than Jennie when I need advice or help with my animals, and, boy, will she tell you if you're doing something wrong!"

My father was a lighthouse keeper and he had a flock of sheep. But he got rid of his, because he couldn't keep them in the pasture, they was always around the lighthouse. That was on Little Nash's Island, right out here about two miles. That's the same island our sheep is on now. We own half of that one and the government owns the other half. And then we own the whole big island, Big Nash's.

Well you see, I spent most of eighteen years out there. And my father got rid of his sheep, and then *we* wanted some, my sister and I. So we asked the fella that had sheep on the big island and we got a cosset —you know, one that the mother wouldn't own. So my sister and I each got one of them cossets and we trained them. When they was little fellas we'd almost live in the pasture with them, see. And when they grew up, we had no problem keeping them in there. Let me see, my sister got married first, and we had thirty-three sheep by then. And I got them. Well, then when I got married, my father give 'em away. But before then, we'd used to harness them up and they'd haul coal. They'd haul carts and sleds, oh yeah!

My father had an old ram with his flock, three of us used to sit up on his back, take a dish of corn and hold it out in front and whenever we wanted to go, we'd shake it. He'd go whatever direction that corn sits, then we'd stop every once in a while and give him a little bit. And when my father sold that ram to the fella that had the big island, that fella said that when he took him home—this makes you feel some bad, did us anyway—he said that ram was so homesick, he said he tied him in every kind of grass, clover, every kind of feed, and that ram stood right there till he died; never ate a mouthful. Well what he did, he missed us kids awful bad. He must have been, oh, eight, nine years old; see, he'd grown right up with us and he just missed us.

Well, anyway, my sister and I started raisin sheep. Then when we moved—I sure *wish* I'd've had this island when I got married—I didn't have no place to keep 'em. So I had to sell 'em all, but I kept my two right around here. Didn't have enough land to build a fence or anything, but I'd keep 'em around here and they'd go over to the neighbors, bum a little cookie or somethin!

So . . . so *then* the fella that had this island out here, the Big Nash's—*which* I'd always wanted all my life, and of course *knew* I never could have it, well, it come up for sale. And of course I knew them both well. The old man that had it first and used to have his sheep on there, he died. Then his partner got old and, of course, he was a mail driver. Well, he didn't tend to them at *all*. Would just let them have what lambs they could and go down there once a year to shear them. Well, they was in *quite* fine shape when I got them!

So I told my husband, "I'm goin over to Stevens', see if I can get that island."

He said, "You're crazy, ain't ya?"

I said, "It's better than havin money in the bank." I says, "There's more to it."

Course, there *was* then. But now oh the last five years have been horrible, prices have been way down. So, anyway, we went over there and we bought that island. Oh that island, boy, I've had trouble tryin to keep it! But I tell my husband, "When I *die* you can sell it, but not before. Long as I can get out there, one week a year even . . ."

Of course, I've been awful lucky with gettin help. I was tryin to get my nephew to take over those sheep and he said, "You think I could find somebody, like you do, every time you want somebody to work for you?"

So I says, "Well shear 'em yourself, then, Joe."

But anyway, that's how I got into the sheep business. I've had as high as three hundred head on five islands, I guess it was, but I've had to cut down on it. Well, Dr. Goodale, he died and we had a lease on Johnson Light but then another fella bought it and the lease wasn't no good. Dr. Goodale never went to a lawyer and had it made out so's it would stand, and it wasn't no good. Then, well, I moved the sheep off. Then we had so many dogs on Pond Island, and they'd get in and cut the sheep up. I said, *"No way* I'm gonna have sheep abused." So I moved them off of there too.

I was gonna tell you about the government, cause I tried to get Little Nash's from the government. But the government they give it to the school, so I don't know what's gonna become of it. Probably somebody'll get drowned if they don't know what they doin' out there! It's not like you *know* landin on this island out here; if you don' know what you're doin, you kin mess up—even when you know what you're doin, you kin too! I been into a few messes out there. And I knew about them, but I wasn't, I wasn't thinkin *straight.* You see, now the chop, that don't mount to a thing. But old Mr. Surf, I don't care how powerful you are, he's a lot more powerful! He'll take you wheres he wants you to go.

Oh yes, I sank a boat one time, a seventeen-footer. I'd been—now this is how foolish it was—I went ashore and took two bales of hay in a ten-footer, that little skiff right down there. I landed them and then there was a sheep in trouble. Well, I tried to run my brother down, and I didn't catch him. I wanted him to shoot that sheep for me. See, the gulls had tore her all to pieces. Ah . . . well, then I said to myself, "You old fool, that's *your* responsibility, go ashore and get that gun and go do it yourself." Well, that was a sheep I was partial to, and I was mad about those gulls tearin her up and me havin to do it myself, you understand. And when I went in, well I wasn't paying no attention. My boat's seventeen feet long and I didn't think the sea was breakin off that far. An just before I hit the beach, I looked up behind me and there was a sea comin at me just about as high as that ceilin there!

I said, "Oh girl, you've had it this time!"

So . . . I grabbed the painter and made a run for it. I swear, seems as though I was underwater—I know I *wasn't*, of course—but it seems as though I was underwater so long I wasn't never goin to make it onto that beach. Well, course the boat filled with water. And I tried to haul her up and, well, I couldn't do nothin. She'd come in with the sea, and she'd go off with it. So I shoved her off and I held her there for three hours till the Coast Guard came by and I yelled at them. I was just waiting for a lobster boat to come by and bail her out. She had so much water in her that everything come out of her, tanks, all my bait, pockets, cans, everything come out of her. And that engine, before I come to and found I couldn't haul her out of there, that engine was underwater, I don't know how many times. Well, so I called the Coast Guard in and asked if they'd bail her out so's I could get aboard her, and they did. Well, they tried to start the engine and they couldn't. So they pushed her in to me; oh, I had to go up to my armpits in the water to get her, and they pushed her in. Then about this time, this other fella he come along to see what was goin on.

And I said, "Dougie, you'll probly have to tow me home, cause that engine's been underwater bout four times and the Coast Guard couldn't start it."

So he reached down, give it a pull, first pull he give it, there it went!

By this time, the wind had changed around to the northwest, which was blowing right onto the shore. And a thunderstorm had come up while I was standin there—course, I couldn't get no wetter anyway—and then all my stuff came right up out of the surf, all I had to do was just go pick it up! Last I'd seen it, it was goin towards Flint Island, that sets bout two miles from my island. Then it come right almost back to me! The wind shifted and brought it right back to me. So I was right lucky, all round!

So soon as I got right back to shore, my brother that I was tryin to chase down, he and I went right back out agin and he shot the sheep. It was just hours—well, three hours—that she had to suffer while I was holdin the boat, but just as soon as I got back in the harbor, we went right straight out agin. But that just goes to show that even when you *know* the islands, you kin get yourself in a mess!

Now I'll tell you about this other sheep that I had to kill. I never realized that she loved me so much. Course I didn't think I thought so much of her, but, oh, she was a beautiful animal! But when I'd go off when she was a baby, now this, you listen, this you *ain't* goin to believe, or maybe you will cause you've had sheep: I'd go out to the island, see. This was in September, see, when she was still on a bottle.

My brother'd come down and this was Labor Day, he says, "Let's go out to the island for Labor Day weekend."

And I said, "Oh fine, that'd be dandy."

So I said to my husband—he'd fed the sheep every mornin, you know, so's I wouldn't have to get up so early—I says to Stan, "Now when you want to go somewheres, Stan, well Lizzie will feed her."

Lizzie's my sister. So away I went. Well, the first one when I came back was Lizzie. She flew into me, and boy!

"Well what's the trouble?" I said, "Well what did Poodie"—that sheep's name was Poodie—"what did Poodie do?"

Well, that was just it, she didn't do nothin! She wouldn't touch her bottle, she wouldn't touch her grain, she wouldn't do *nothin*. Just put her head up against the building and sulk. Well, of course, when I got to the house Stan flew into me.

"Well," I said, "what did Poodie do?"

Just the same. Nothin. He says, "She wouldn't even eat her macaroon cookies." She used to love macaroon cookies; I bet she ate ten pounds of them before she died.

I said, "What are you talkin about, Stan? I don't believe, no, that she'd starve herself."

And oh, she was standin right behind me. So I went to reach up over the sink after her bottle and that tail started goin round and round and round, and I fed her that bottle. And, oh, she went at it! Course, she hadn't had nothin, cause she wouldn't drink. And Stan passed her a cookie and she turned her nose up.

I said, "Let me have that."

He passed it to me and of course, she ate it like it was goin out of style. Well so that settled that little episode. Then come November and I went out birdin, out to our camp out there on the island.

And when I came back, my brother says, "You know, that thing won't eat her grain."

And of course I was just blowin, you know, tryin to be funny, and I says, "You know what the trouble is?" I says, "I haven't had time for her to kiss her mother."

Well, I stuck my head in over the fence there, just foolishly, like I didn't think she'd—well, she went right to one side of me and licked me from this ear to the other and then went right straight into her grain!

And he jumped right up and down, my brother did, and said, "That's the—!"

Oh dear! Course, I loved that old sheep. I did, and then that's the one the dogs tore up. I told Pop, I wouldn't even go to hall that day, it tore me up so bad. And now if I ever meet that dog, course I'm not a cruel person, but it has never left me, that horrible feeling has never left me . . . if I could catch that dog, if I could shoot him, I would.

Now I've got one sheep out here that my sister's got quite partial to. Rocky. And I don't know why everbody loves him. Last fall, I put him out on the island cause he was bad, see, he wouldn't stay in the pasture. So I put him out on the island. Course, break your heart, it'll really break your heart cause he don't think he's a sheep in the beginning. And he don't want a sheep to touch him. An I put him on that island, and he *howled* to come back home with us. It was awful! So my niece Judy starts in.

She says, "When you goin to go get Rocky?"

I says, "Aw, I don' knows as I will."

She says, "If you don't, I'm goin to git Joe to git him."

That's her husband and they think Rocky is just about *it*. Joe buys him caramels. Just here a while ago, he says, "You know, Rocky'd only eat one caramel. You know that's funny."

I said, "Is it, Joe? By any chance you didn't give one of the other sheep any, did you?"

"Oh yes," he says, "there was another sheep come there and I give her some."

I said, "There's your trouble, right there. Rocky was mad." Oh, he's as jealous as can be! No, Rocky doesn't think he's a sheep. He more or less thinks he's a person.

There's people think sheep is so dumb. They'll say how when one jumps into the ocean, they all will. I argue this out.

"Well now," I says, "you think sheep are stupid. Well what about your people?"

And they'll say, "Well what do you mean?"

I says, "Well you get a fire goin in a place where there's a lot of people and they'll kill more gittin out than what the fire will. Well now," I says, "what's the difference? They're scared. And that's the way with the sheep. The sheep is frightened, if she wasn't, she wouldn't jump into the water. That's the last thing she would do. So now," I says, "why is a sheep any stupider than people?"

Lot of them fires, they say there was more killed trampled to death. I see that over here at Millbridge, I mean it was so foolish. They had a little electric fire, and somebody hollered "Fire!" My goodness, they jumped out through the windows! And we had a little old lady with us, I guess she just got right down on her knees and crawled right through everybody's legs, cause she was out through that door before anybody else was! Well, I just stood up and looked around to see what was goin on. They were all afraid. And it wasn't but just startin to smoke, wasn't anything at all. And I thought then, they tell about how sheep is foolish!

There was nine kids in my family. Seven boys and two girls. You wonder why I am the way I am? Growin up with all them rough-houses? I don' know how my poor mother stood it! I think of it now. I think of it now, because let me take somebody with me in the boat, kids 'specially, well, it really bothers me. I'm right on the alert all the time, with them kids, whether they're goin to get overboard or some-thin. Somethin's goin to happen. Really, that's just the same as goin out here in the fog. Now I don't mind it, goin my husband and I, but when there's somebody with me, oh, oh, oh boy I rather take a—because there's always that chance you kin booboo. That would be the time that you would!

But you see, ever since I was ten year old, I been messing around in a boat. I had ten lobster traps when I was ten years old. Course, we liked to get in them pods and go get the wood over on the other island, thought that was a big deal, you know. A pod's a boat that's pointy on both ends, like a canoe. Well, we'd fill them pods just as full of wood! An then I got my mother on top of a load one day, she was so scared! It was the tricky pod, too; we had two pods, one tricky and one not. The tricky one was almost like a canoe, you'd jest put your foot up on one side like that, she'd flop right down and put water in her. That was the one I used to fish in, I fished out lobster traps, used to go right around the island. My father and sister would go out in the big boat, the big pod.

Course, we had to go to school too. We started out havin a teacher out there on the island. And we'd get in, well maybe, *possibly* four weeks out of the year. This teacher'd go from island to island, two weeks here, two weeks there. By the time she got back to our island, we'd already forgot what she'd learned us. Then she'd go home and one of my brothers'd propose. That's what kept happenin to 'em. My seven brothers took to marryin 'em fast as they come on the island. I think it was Raymond who got the last one they ever sent us.

Then they sent us up to Portland to go to school. And the whole term I don't think I got more than perhaps two weeks again. I was sick the whole time. An I got home, I had a cough you'd have thought was T.B. Well, I was home three days and never seen it since! Well you see, we was used to doin, like we'd go out and get soakin wringin wet and all that foolishness. Didn't bother us. We'd either hang our clothes on the rocks and get 'em dry, 'specially if we'd been doin somethin bad like gettin caught between the two islands and the tide come in up around us! Like we did, we was tryin to get two yearlings across there one time, my sister and I. We got them halfway across and they blocked on us. We couldn't get them one way or the other, and the tide started comin in. So we stayed with 'em, then we swum 'em back to shore. Then we didn't dare go up to the house and tell Mother, so we took all of our clothes off and dried them on the rocks!

Course that stuff, Mother never knew, *never* knew. So you know, you was bound to get into these little bit of messes, you know. And I don't know why she didn't go crazy. I suppose she was kinda relyin on the older ones takin care of the younger ones, I don't know. I always was my father's girl, really. Mother and I got on like cats and dogs . . . Well, cats and dogs'd get along *better*, really.

Well, anyway, then the government said we had to be in school over here on the mainland. By that time, I was round thirteen, and of course they put us back cause we never really had much schoolin—you know, it was a different kind of teachin out on the island altogether.

We were sent over here and there was just one family that ever used us decent and the rest of them just made fun of us. Course, we was different, havin lived on an island.

So one day, I got up and I said, "I'm goin home." I said, "I've had enough of those children, that's enough for me."

So I go on the boat and away I went.

Mother said, "You're goin back to school!"

"Mother," I said, "you kin send me back to school. I'll go back to the highland. But I'll never set foot in that schoolhouse again."

"Well," she said, "you're a-goin."

I said, "No, I'm not. You kin send me back. I'll go. But *never* am I settin foot in that schoolhouse agin!" So we won, my sister and I.

I'll tell you what the trouble was. They had the idea that my father was rich cause he had that job. Course he wasn't rich, cause there was nine of us then, and he only made around fifty dollars a month. The idea was, they was more envious than anything else. They was just kids, just miserable kids. Well, we was just different, just different, that's all there was to it. And kids can be awful cruel.

So then I started lobster fishin and I did that till I was almost twenty-one. Then I got married an was away from fishin for about ten years. I got married in January and I was twenty-one in March; that was back in nineteen thirty-three. My husband and I, we cut wood, he hauled wood and worked on the roads. He was road commissioner. And I've worked all kinds of jobs. You name it, and I've done it. But then after ten years, we started fishin agin.

Now let's see, I've got one, two, three skiffs, and a pod, and an outboard. So I'm boat-poor, really. But I can't seem to, there's none of them I can get rid of, there's a time I have a use for all of them. Yeah, I'm boat-poor, that's right!

Mostly I've lobster-fished, but I also went fishin with my brother. He had a drag boat an I went fishin one year with him.

I said, "Bubba, will you tell me what in the world you want me to go with you for?" I said, "I'm jest an old . . ."

Yeah, he rigged up all kinds of rigs for me to get in over the boat, cause I was lame then. And he said that was the only time that he ever dragged and he didn't have somebody bitchin aboard. There was always one that didn't want to do the dishes, an one that didn't want to do the cookin, an one . . . There was my nephew and this other fella from Bath on that year. Oh, didn't they use to raise the devil with me! And we did have a good time! I'd do it another year, yes, I would. It's really exciting. We caught a halibut, an just his head weighed thirty pounds! Course, we was always bettin how many halibut there was goin to be. And this time we'd dropped the net and we'd only dragged forty-five minutes an that net got what we call "mudded her down."

And I said, "Oh boy, there's that old halibut I been tellin you we're going to get!"

Bubba says, "Oh, I like to hear you talk, but your judgment's awful poor!"

That net was just as full of mud, and there that halibut was, with just his head stickin out. You talk about an excited crowd—it weighed more than two hundred pounds!

There's a friend of mine, another woman who goes lobstering too. I don't know why the others don't. It's not hard. Except for those ten years, I've been at it every year since I was a girl. I guess it's like a fever with me. It gets into your blood, lobster-fishin does. And water does. Oh my gosh yes, the old ocean, it *gets* you, there's no question about it!

I'm lamed up but I'll keep on a-doin it. I'll stay on the water as long as I can, I guess. An like I've told Stan, he can sell the island when I'm dead, but not before. As long as I'm around, I'll have that island.

Jack-of-All-Trades
Eleanor Johnson

Eleanor Johnson lives in New York state. A would-be landscape architect and forester whose father thought that an unsuitable occupation for a girl, Eleanor has transformed a crumbling farm into a showplace. There must be fifteen acres of landscaped woodlands around the house, so artfully done it takes a while to realize how much work such seemingly natural beauty represents. Inside the farmhouse, hooked rugs, handmade quilts, antique furniture polished to a glow, seem more like a decorator's dream than what they are, the work of Eleanor's hands.

For the last thirty years, Eleanor has shared the farmhouse with her cousin, Frances, who was one of the first women doctors graduated from Columbia Medical School. She retired from the active practice of medicine two years ago, at the age of eighty.

"The next time you write to me," Eleanor chastised me, "don't say you want to talk to old women. Put an 'er' on the end of it, please. They've given me no end of a hard time since you called me that!"

I had a camp for girls up in northern Michigan. And then during the war, I did recreation for USO, and traveled all over the country setting up all the recreation in all of the camps. I mean, stuff I didn't know at all! I thoroughly enjoyed it, but I worked very hard. At that time, I thought that it would be nice to have a place in the East. So I started looking out from New York City, with the man I was engaged to at that time. We thought that we would have a coed camp. But then he was killed in the war, and so I just kept on coming up and looking by myself. And I found this place. It had a pond and barns that I thought I could use for dormitories, and so on. So I bought it, which was very cheap. And I didn't have any money, but I made a down payment and then gradually paid for it.

After the war then I had a lot of writing to do and I had accepted a position with the national YWCA in charge of recreation. But I also had to write up a summary of everything that had happened in recreation during the war. Well, I had bought this place and I was supposed to write that all up, so I came up here and saw all the things I wanted to do. The house was a mess, you know. This was all solid *mildew* and trees growing right up in front, no lawn, nothing in back. The house was built around seventeen ninety and no one had lived here for thirty years, so it was really in bad condition. I had close to two hundred acres then, I just have one hundred and thirty left now. I had to sell seventy acres when the parkway came through.

Anyway, I went down to Manhattan to my apartment and finished the writing. And then I resigned. And I had hardly started at the Y! But I *knew* this was what I wanted to do. And I didn't want to have charge of other people's children anymore. I decided, I was going to see if I could just possibly make this farm pay for itself. Which I couldn't! I had *never* been around sheep or lived in the country, really, except for my camp. And there was so much to do, like I got through painting the barns—which *I* did—and then I did get sheep and I kept on getting them until I had sixty-five ewes and a couple of rams. And then I'd have—well, hopefully sixty-five lambs!—but a lot of 'em had twins so . . .

Well, first of all, when I got this place, I discovered I'd *inherited* an old man! Who lived here and at another place up the hill. And he drank as he breathed! When I tried to clean out this well, it was full of empty beer bottles! Completely full. When I came, there was only that well and the water that goes over the little waterfall out there. And there was no electricity. There was just a Delco system which hadn't been used for all those years, you know, a gas generator. So I sold the Delco and connected up to the Rural Electrification. Then I had to see that all the wires were safe, because they were wires that had gone to a DC system. And so . . . I don't know how I did what I did! I can't possibly imagine. I lived alone, and I heated with this fireplace and the stove out there. I took up the floors, I put down floors, I painted, I—I don't know how I did it! Of course, there were times I thought I was crazy to be doing it, but I had already done a house up in Michigan.

I bought a place there where the camp was when I was first out of college, when I was about eighteen. I skipped grades and I went through college in three years but—I mean, I had already skipped the eighth grade and a couple grades—*not* that I was smart; they just bumped me through! So, I had *always* wanted to take landscape gardening and be a forester. I wanted to do forestry *and* landscape gardening. And I went to the state university and started in taking forestry, but the foresters all had to go to a camp for the summer, and I was the only girl in the forestry school. And when my father heard about that, he wouldn't have *anything* to do with it. So he stopped that and I just went on in the liberal arts course.

And I had never even tried to hit a nail, I don't think, until I bought this place in northern Michigan. I was only eighteen when I got it, and I thought that it was just the most wonderful place. I had saved a thousand dollars and the man who owned it committed suicide, and I had a chance to buy ninety-eight acres with five hundred old apple trees and five hundred young apple trees and a hundred pear trees on it for a thousand dollars! And do you know that my sister sold it a few years ago for almost two hundred thousand dollars? Now they've put up condominiums and it breaks my heart to go up there.

It had an old house on it too and an old fallen-down barn, and quite a bit of lake frontage. Well that lake was one of the most beautiful lakes in the world—at least they said that in *National Geographic,* and I really think it *is* beautiful! And everyone told me I should tear the house down, it was in such bad shape. But I thought I could fix it up. So I tore out two partitions, without ever knowing that the whole house could fall down if you took out two partitions! Nobody helped me. *I* did this. Luckily enough, they weren't bearing walls, and I made a big living room by taking out two partitions. And I drove down a new well over on the other side of the kitchen. And the floor there, they'd put apples on that kitchen floor and it had rotted right down to the basement. So I had to put a new floor, and then the roof leaked! It was just so bad. You wouldn't *dream,* what I did about the roof! I don't know how I even knew that shingles or roll roofing should overlap going down; I guess I *did* have sense to know the rain would have to go that way. But I did the dumbest thing! I just had one ladder, I'd never heard of a hook ladder that hooks over the ridge of the roof, and I never thought of a scaffolding. But I put the first roll of roofing on standing on a ladder leaning up against the house. I followed all the directions, you know, put tar on the nails, and so on. Then when it came to the second row, I had a terrible time. This was a steep roof, and I didn't know how you were supposed to *stay* on the roof! So I poured down a puddle of tar and sat in it, to *stick* myself to the roof! You know, I had the sorest behind anybody ever saw, *bright* red! Oh, was it sore! Well, anyway, I did the whole roof this way, sitting in puddles of tar!

And then after I took down those partitions, I had to put up wallboard and I didn't know how to put it up on the ceiling. I didn't know anything about a deadman to hold it up; I've found these things out since. But! What I did was I put the nails in one end of the board like this, and I took a broom and I held it up while I worked my hand back like this, and got one nail in, then I moved the broom a little and got one more nail in. Well, finally I got the whole ceiling up, without ever really having anything to hold it up! *Then* there were some cracks, but that's when I learned to put tape across them. Well, *that* covers a *multitude* of sins!

The ceiling in *this* house was all coming down when I got it, too. Absolutely rotten. And I put wallboard all in here, but I never did get it perfect. There is *nothing* square in this house! So you have to make an *illusion*. If you put anything up, you have to stand back and see, "Now, should it go this way, or that?" I've papered every bit of this house; you stand with a plumb line, and then you think, it *has* to line up with the doorframe. If you get the illusion right, it ends up looking quite straight. I mean, you don't notice that this is all off, do you?

Anyway, I got that place in Michigan and was going to have an orchard. But the next year I was there, it went down to forty-eight degrees below zero, with hardly any snow on the ground, and I could hear those apple trees out there cracking from *end* to *end*. They just cracked through and died. So I knew I couldn't make a go of that. And furthermore, my family is a very . . . they think what belongs to one belongs to everybody. Well, one time I had a house party. I had divided the loft upstairs with sheets and the girls slept on one side and the boys on the other. Well, in the midst of this, up comes my mother with a club that she belonged to.

And I said to her, "*Mother,* I love to have you come, but I wish you'd give me the privilege of inviting you!"

And she was so hurt she wouldn't speak to me for a couple of weeks! So after that, I thought, "Oh what the heck, I can't fight this!" So I decided to start a camp. And I thought I would do it for poor kids. Factory kids, and they can't afford even to go to the YW camps. So I went around and I decided if I just charged them seven dollars a week, that would do it. And we'd put up tents and they'd help with the garden and it'd be *good* for them, do the dishes and so on, and it'd be *theirs* too. I ended up with fifty-seven kids, most of whom couldn't've paid for a private camp. But we had an awfully good time! I got my sister to come help me with it. We'd been to camps for years, so we knew. And then, we made the kids do everything. And they did, they worked the garden, we took canoe trips . . . and then I knew a man who loaned us a whole string of polo ponies.

I nearly wore myself to a frazzle, I was so afraid one of those kids would be hurt. But after that, we raised the prices and made it a regular camp. We just turned it into a private camp, which was quite successful. And then finally I didn't want to go on with it anymore and my sister did, so I sold it to her. I decided I *never* wanted a camp again. I'd never be responsible for other people's children.

So I got this place, using all my money, which at that time was nothing really. And there was this old man here, that was *such* a character. He wrote poetry and his name was Billy. He had white hair, and blue eyes, and he played the zither. I could have company, and he'd be up on the hill playing the zither the whole time! But one time, he came at night, he knocked on the door. He had on a top hat, had on a swallowtailed coat, a white vest, a cane with an alligator on the top. Takes off his hat and he bows, and I looked and he had on rouge and lipstick and a false mustache.

He said, "Feel these goods."

I said, "Well, Billy, those are good goods, where did you get them?"

And he said, "Oh, up in the barn here, they gave me these old clothes. I'm going down to show the boys."

So I knew he was going down to drink like anything down in town. But that's the kind of man he was, he'd put on rubber faces and stick his head in at the window. Oh yes, he was born right here, and his family before him. He was quite a character. Imagine me coming here and not knowing anything about this country at all, and having this false face pop up at your windows! Every window I put nails in because he'd come with his whole gang and yell and holler about three o'clock in the morning and pound on the doors!

Well, anyway, after him, I started getting a few animals in. Like I had fifty chickens. And then Frances and I—she's my cousin, you see—

we decided that we'd try it together up here for a year and see how we got along. And she's been here ever since. She's eighty-two and she just stopped practicing medicine a few years ago!

Then I had another old man who was a farmer. His name was Harry and he'd had six children. Then his wife died of scarlet fever, so Harry gave his six farms to his six children and started working for other people and drinking. So I got him to come and help me, and fifty cents an hour was all he'd take! Which was more than I had too, really. But anyway, I started buying sheep then, good ones that I could find. I didn't have any fences and I had to go up in the woods and cut posts. And I got another farmer up here to help me and we made an old doodlebug out of an old Ford—a doodlebug is instead of a tractor, which I couldn't afford, and it did almost what a tractor would do. This farmer and I made it.

I cleared out maybe twenty acres up here, which I fenced in sections so I could move the sheep from one section to another. Around the house was all sheep, and across the road was too. So I got the sheep, and oh, I had a wonderful ram, just a wonderful ram! So my sheep really got top prices. Anyway, Harry was starting to help me to get the hay in the first year, and then he had a brain tumor and went out of his head. He started to work here in his pajamas then, and Frances said, "I simply will *not* have a man haying out here in his pajamas!"

And Harry says to me, "I don't know what's the matter with her! She's just like my son. I wanted to go swimmin and there were some women there and I had on my long underwear that covered me from here down to here, and my son wouldn't let me go in swimmin with them in my underwear! And he came and he brought me a pair of shorts, they weren't *that* long, and I didn't have anything here or here, and *that* was all right!''

Well, anyway, his son took him to be operated on and he never came back. In the meantime, I got in all the haying all by myself. I cut it with a one-horse mowing machine, and then I brought it in on a lop-sided hayrack! And I learned how to load a hayrack. It's really something—you have to put it on like a thatch roof, put each bundle on and overlap it. Everyone around me had tractors and modern equipment by then. But someone told me about a hayfork. Old Harry, before he went, showed me how to use a hayfork and we went to some old farmer and got one. And I filled that barn to the top with hay, all by myself. I don't know how I did it, but I did! See, he taught me things like winnowing the windrows. You cut the hay and then you rake it into a win'row, and then you rake it together—by hand!—and then you take your hayfork and lift it up onto your wagon and bring it in.

Meanwhile, I had an eighth of an acre of raspberries I'd put in all along here, and I had to get up at the crack of dawn and pick them, and go down to town and sell them. Forty quarts of raspberries I picked every morning! And meantime, every night I was doing something in the house. Fixing it up, or making rugs. I made all the rugs for the house to begin with. Either braided or hooked. And making quilts. Or doing clay, I did quite a few ceramic things and I could sell them. I did those just to sell, which would bring me in a little money. I wasn't working, and I had never lived before without working. My father thought that this was just terrible, he really objected strenuously; my whole family did. To me coming East by myself from Michigan and living here, with the war that was on.

I had fifty chickens and I sold all the eggs in town. And I had, oh

I don't know how many ducks, I had ducks all over the place, which I raised and sold. And I had geese, and I had pigs. I only had four pigs. I decided that if I had four pigs, I could have one to keep that would be for us to eat, one to keep to breed if there happened to be a really good sow, and the other two I would sell; and that would pay for ours, our two would be free. So I did that, but only just for one year. Because after the pigs were sold, this one beautiful sow was left and she was *tremendous,* she weighed several hundred pounds. She'd be up there alone and a half an hour later, she was right here. She'd figured how to get out. They are the smartest animals there are! So I pegged up the hole. Well, that was good for an hour. Well, I did any number of things to stop her, but finally I decided, "Oh, let her just come down." So she would pick up a stick and the dog would chase her, and she would drop the stick and dog would pick it up, so then she would chase him! Every time I'd take a walk, she'd follow me. If I was painting the barn, she'd pay no attention to the ladder until I was up it, then she'd scratch her back on it. Well, she got so big and so familiar that I knew we couldn't keep her. And I would never butcher her, so I sold her to a farmer that wanted to raise pigs and I didn't ever do that again!

So old Harry had left—I'm not even beginning to tell you how funny these handymen were, they were real characters! And then meantime, I had a big vegetable garden, and I was doing the house, and the sheep and the pigs, ducks, the geese, *and* Banty hens—I don't know how I ever did all that!—and I painted everything that is painted, I papered everything inside.

So next, I got an Italian who lived up here to come and stay. And he stayed in the back of the barn, there's a room fixed up there. And he couldn't read or write, none of these men could. He swore all the time. Charlie, he was a big northern Italian with blue eyes and a big walrus mustache. Well, the idea was that he'd watch the sheep at night and I'd watch them in the daytime, cause I didn't want to get up in the night. I wanted them to lamb in February, which is the dead of winter here, so we'd have Easter lamb. I had the barn all rigged up with lights, so the lambs could get under the lights and keep warm. I had it all divided up so the ewes that were due to lamb were in one part, and I had a sliding window so I could sit there and watch the ewe lambing and stay fairly warm. Then the ewes that were next were in the next pen, and the ones with quite a ways to go were at the far end of the barn.

So, Charlie would come down and he'd say, "Oh! Miss Johnson! Eleanor! Eleanor! I beg you on bended knee, you come, you come. She suffer, she suffer, oh my God, how she suffer!" he'd say. "OOOOOOH! How she suffer!"

I'd say, "Listen, she's just having a lamb, just let nature take its course."

"Oh, no, she suffer, oh my God, how she suffer!"

This was in the middle of the night, night after night. So I'd go up there, I couldn't resist it. And she would just be having a lamb.

"Oh my God, she suffer, you help, you help!"

That one year, I delivered thirty-two lambs, more than any other year! I must say, though, a few were breech births, and I didn't lose a one. But what he would do, as soon as the lamb was born, he'd dash with a dirty old burlap bag and wipe it off—"It's gonna freeze, it's gonna freeze!"—he'd take *all* the smell off it, so the mother couldn't identify her lamb anymore.

So I'd say, "Charlie, you stop it now!" They *had* to smell their lambs and they had to lick them. "They'll get them warm, anyway, we're going to put them in the pen with the lamps there."

"Oh, no! They freeze!"

Well, I just had a terrible time with that, and some of the mothers, new mothers, would butt the lambs and try to get rid of them. I had more cosset lambs up here in front of the fireplace, feeding them with Coca-Cola bottles and nipples because of that! Well, I finally got him to stop doing it. But of course, it was way below zero lots of times when we were lambing. And then I went up every two hours all night long. That was the only thing I could do, because he would come and just, "Ooooooh, I beg you, on bended knee, I beg you!"

I had never even touched a sheep before I got those. I was so surprised a sheep was hard, I thought it was going to be soft! Oh, I read a lot, that's mostly how I learned.

Dogs got in and killed, that's when I stopped raising them, that's what stopped me. But that wasn't my tragedy. I don't remember what year it was, somewhere around nineteen sixty. What happened to me was that I had loaned a ram to a man down the road. One day I thought I'd go down and see how the ram's getting along. And when I got down, his sheep looked simply terrible—the wool coming out, and everything.

I said to him, "What's the matter with your sheep?"

"Nothing, they have ticks."

"Well," I said, "I'm going to take the ram back."

He was one I was particularly fond of. And so I took him and put him in the horse stall. He was crazy about the horse anyway. They loved each other. So I put him in there, and I called the vet. And I said, "What's the matter with this ram?"

"Oh," he said, "it's just ticks and you can't spray until it's warmer."

Well, I didn't believe him. And I read the bulletin and it looked like scabies to me. I told the vet this and he said, "There hasn't been any scabies in New York state for fifty years. So it can't be that."

Well, to make an awfully long story short, after two vets told me it wasn't anything but ticks, I let the ram in with the ewes. Then they all started to lose their wool and they all had this. So I had another vet come out and take scrapings and it *was* scabies.

He said, "You're quarantined as of this moment! You must not sell a lamb or let a lamb off of this property. Where did you get it?"

So I told him and the vet went down there, but that farmer had already sold all his sheep! So here I was quarantined all winter, with farm experts coming from Turkey, from all over the world, to see my *horrible* sheep! It just about broke my heart. And they were miserable, the wool came out and I knew there wouldn't be any wool crop. Then they said in the spring I had to dip all the sheep in this stuff to kill the scabies. So the time came, and I had all the sheep and the water ready with that stuff in it, and I was all by myself. And the agriculture people who had said that they would help came dressed up in business suits.

I said, "Who's going to help me?"

"Oh, we're going to help hold the stop watch," they said.

You had to keep each sheep in the dip two minutes and put its head under water twice before you let it out. Well, I started in, and you know to put sheep in a dip, and put their heads under, and hold them there for two minutes, well, I did about forty sheep and I was *exhausted*. Totally exhausted. And I turned to those men there and said, "If you're not going to help me, you get the hell off of this place!" So they stood there outside somewhere, because they were supposed to be watching and I went on. Then I looked at the lambs. The lambs started to nurse and in about ten minutes, convulsions. Almost every lamb there was dead from nursing. I had asked, "Is it safe to put the lambs in with them?"

"Oh, yes! Just put them in."

So then I said they had to pay me for every lamb that was dead.

"Oh, no, the state doesn't have any money to pay for that."

I said that I would sue.

And he said, "You won't get anywhere if you do, because there isn't a bit of money allocated to pay for something like that. But just look at it this way, you've taught us something."

So I had to do all this again in ten days. And that time, I didn't put the lambs with them for three days. And then dogs got in right after that too, and killed some of them. And that was when I stopped. That was just the end as far as I was concerned.

But this is what old Charlie was like. One day I had a lot of company coming and I said, "Charlie, there's going to be a lot of children here and you will *please* watch your language. Don't you go and swear in front of them."

And he said, "Oh, all right."

Well, there was a pile of bricks up by the barn and after they had been here for a few hours, he came down and he says, "I had to bawl those kids out."

I said, "Well, Charlie, why?"

"They're breaking up the bricks. They found a hammer and they are breaking up all the bricks! But I didn't bawl 'em out hard. I just said to 'em, 'By Jesus, if you little sons of bitches don't stop this, I'm going to break your so-and-so's!'" He says, "Miss Johnson, I didn't bawl them out hard!"

Oh, he was a character!

The sheep paid the taxes and the bills for the place, the electricity and the fuel, and things like that. And the chickens always more than paid for themselves. But if you ever got in the county agent to advise you, you wouldn't want to ever do anything, they're so discouraging! You can't do this or that, that won't ever make money! They just discourage you. In those days, they weren't interested in little people like us. This is dairy country, you see. No one had sheep.

I built the dip I put those sheep in. Oh, that wasn't hard to do . . . but what did I do that was hard? I can't *imagine* having all those raspberries, and all those potatoes and . . . *wheeling* them up here with a plain wheelbarrow, and cutting hay, at the same time having all those sheep and chickens and ducks, and . . . and I didn't really have anybody, you see after Harry and Charlie. And then I had a man came in by the day, but he dropped dead, and that's another story.

But, oh, I think there have been women like me from the beginning of time. I think that—you know, my ancestors were pioneers, they started out down the Hudson. The next generation left and went to Rochester, had a mill and did the first newspaper there. Next generation went to Michigan and they cleared the land and built a place; and then the next generation was mine and *they* went out to the West Coast. So I don't even have quite the pioneer spirit that some of them do. But, really, I don't know why I am . . . because my family is all musical, and I'm not a bit. I talked to my sister the other day, and she said, "I helped someone paper a room and I'd never papered before in my life; I couldn't believe how hard it is!" And we grew up together and everything!

But I always just liked to do things for myself, and I always just loved trees and nature. When I used to be in college, I'd just walk by myself, and walk, and walk. I liked it. I like nature and I like to do things with my hands. I'm not really good at anything, I'm just sort of a jack-of-all-trades.

IV

LOOKING AHEAD

A Beautiful Life
Marion Welsh and Marie Copp

Marion Welsh operates what is one of the top dairy herds in Vermont. Not only is her milk production high, but every inch of her farm is tended and cared for in a way that is no longer common. Her partner and friend, Marie Copp, for years raised the young calves and still grows the garden that is a principal source of their food.

Marion and Marie met at a small college in Pennsylvania where Marie was a professor and Marion a student. Their friendship grew through two years of operating a faculty/student summer program on Marie's farm in Connecticut. Eventually, they went into business together, operating a dairy farm. Marion is now in her fifties, and Marie in her seventies. Like other "small" farmers today, they face many economic difficulties and questions about the viability of their type of farming.

Marion: The *green* is what brought me to Vermont. It looked to us like Vermont was more productive per square inch, in spite of the short growing season, than anyplace else we'd seen. The weather here varies a lot. There's *nothing* predictable about the weather in Vermont, except that it always rains when you've got hay on the ground!

We had a small farm in Connecticut that Marie had inherited from her family, but it got so crowded down there that it became untenable to stay and try to farm, so we came up here.

Marie: We came to Vermont and decided on the purchase of the original farm where the barn still is, and the little house across the way. But we had no house for ourselves, so we bought the adjacent farm too. Then we brought all our cows up from Connecticut, about seventy head with the young cows, and all our equipment, and we settled in the farmhouse on the second farm we bought.

Marion: We got the first cow up in Connecticut to help feed us, and one cow just sort of led to another. We've had as many as one hundred milkers up here. For years, we ran two fifty-cow dairies on the two farms here. It's only been in the last five or six years that we have had just the one dairy. It was always inconvenient to have two herds in two places, but it just got so it seemed the help situation was nearly impossible and we cut back to one dairy. And I think the per-cow production has been better since we did that, because we can concentrate more on them.

We are considered an old-fashioned, obsolete kind of farm. We only have fifty cows, we milk in bucket milkers, we have no pipeline, we have no milking parlor. And we don't have huge tractors. We have one big tractor that is heavy enough to do our heaviest work. And we still do things more or less—well, we are considered old-fashioned. Today, one person should be doing all this alone with a lot of very expensive equipment. No one talks about how all this technology replaces human labor. And then we end up feeding people who have no work. If we had a *real* agricultural policy in this country, of save the soil, work the land, *and* employ the people, it wouldn't be *nearly* so costly. But all they can see is short-run dollar signs. Labor-intensive agriculture would be a *big* help to this society, but we've gone by it, and I don't think you can turn it around.

I think the help situation is one of the biggest problems that you have if you have to hire outside help. And I think that's one place where being a woman may be a problem. I've never thought of it as a *big* problem, but I think it is *a* problem—I'm sure of that. Well, I've only had one man that I had to fire because he blatantly wouldn't take orders from a woman and he also wouldn't keep his hands off—I often have women working for me. He was the only one that I had to fire for that mentality. But there's a resistance, just a *resistance*. There's no getting around it.

Marie: Even if it's unconscious, it's still there . . .

Marion: As a woman . . . I think you have a little harder time getting *through* to them. But I've had some really good help too. I think I've had a lot of cooperation from men help over the years. It hasn't been a big problem.

The *big* problem has been a problem about getting money. When we were in Connecticut, we had the backing and support of the farm machinery man, of course, because he could see all kinds of chances to sell farm machinery. And Marie had some stock for collateral, otherwise I'm sure we wouldn't have gotten a *cent*, because the notion of two women farming, they didn't want any part of that!

As recently as a few years ago, we were going to sell this farm and buy one somewhere else. We had a buyer and he went to the FHA and had no trouble at all being financed on this fine farm and this fine dairy with this fine equipment. And then the deal fell through and we thought, "Well, we'll take this fine equipment and this fine dairy to the FHA and get financed there to *our* advantage." And then all of a sudden, they didn't want us anymore. The man who had wanted to buy it was an inexperienced farmer too! And then we heard by way of the grapevine that they turned us down because we were women.

That's been a problem, I *know* it's been a problem. I think it's still a problem as far as our local bank is concerned. More recently, we again approached the FHA and now they will loan us money and it may be now because we *are* women. But being a woman is a problem as far as the finances go, and that's a big problem, because you can't run a farm without some kind of cash flow, some line of credit.

We talked to a banker just last week who said that fifty cows is the smallest dairy that he will even *talk* to. I think this is too bad. I still think that a very fine dairy handled by a family, couple women, couple men, I don't care what, but where you don't have to hire a lot of help, a dairy of thirty, thirty-five really top cows will do all right. But there's a very very strong feeling today that if you don't get bigger, you should get out. It's a kind of thinking I think is very dangerous.

We're at the tail end of the world up here in Vermont. Energy's going to get scarce, and it's going to get expensive. We truck what we produce here *out* of the state, we truck what we eat back into the state. It doesn't make any sense at all, you know. But you talk of diversifying, of trying to grow more of our own food here, and they say it won't work. . . . There *are* economic problems with diversifying, with growing more small crops, but I believe that New England could be self-sufficient in food, and that it had better be! You hear these same old platitudes, "We've got to keep our lands open, keep Vermont rural," but nobody *means* it, you know what I mean? A lot of words and they aren't going to keep Vermont rural or agriculture viable with a lot of platitudes.

This state is really promoting industry at the same time as they're saying "Preserve our agriculture lands." How can they do both? Where are all the people from those industries in Burlington going to live? They're going to live right here in Hinesburg. And I don't think we can save the farms, short of buying up the development rights. If we took some action *now* in Vermont to buy up development rights on large-enough tracts of land for there to be viable farms left, I think something could be done. But the state says it's not rich enough to do it. And the public would have to think it's a priority. Usually, places like Massachusetts and Long Island, where they have done it, they don't get around to it until they're down to their last five thousand acres of land. And probably that is what will happen here in Vermont too. The number of farms is going down very fast and very steadily. Land is going out of production in Vermont at the rate of two hundred acres per day!

Some of the big farmers in the Midwest worry me because I think they're not concerned about their soils. I sympathize with farmers and all their problems, and everything else, but I don't have too much sympathy with farmers that *know* their topsoil is leaving at a rate of six or seven inches a year. And who don't do any of the conservation practices they could to save it. They don't rotate their crops, and they don't do the things to conserve the land. And I'm very concerned about the use of herbicides and pesticides and things like that. It's such a short-sighted thing! We have to do something different. I don't think things are that bad here yet, partly because there isn't enough room to get so big. There've been times when I've thought, "After all, there's so much farmland out there, who needs New England?"

Now and then I get disgusted and think, "Well, why keep fighting? Let it go, cash it in and let it go, cause there's all that farmland out there. Let people live here, people have to have someplace to live."

But I think parts of the West are going to become a dust bowl again if they don't do something about it. The water supply is running out. They're worried about oil. And my feeling is that there's a lot of water in New England, and on the small plots of land here you can grow a *lot* of food. You could grow all the food for the town of Hinesburg on thirty acres of good farmland here. And I feel that our smaller tracts of really good soil, which we don't have all that much of, should *not* just be written off as inessential.

I've been thinking about selling raw milk at some sort of farmers' market. But it needs capitalizing. And we always seem to be hurting for money. If you *had* something to start with, you wouldn't always be paying interest on money that you didn't have. We *started* with borrowed money and . . . well, something like a raw milk operation that would take a lot of capitalization, the commercial banks around here couldn't care less about. They are about as innovative and as interested in agri-culture as . . . well, they don't even want to talk to farmers anymore.

But it would be nice. It would be nice to see a neat little market right across the road from the barn, and see my own milk. I'd want to bottle in glass, because that's the only decent way to keep milk. I almost think the way to make a farmers' market work would be for one farmer to own the market, a farmer that is dedicated to using locally grown products, and run it as a business with one person running it, to try to make a reasonable profit. "Yes, I'd be happy to get your tomatoes, and your corn, and if you have bees, I want your honey, and your maple syrup. . . ." I think that could be done. When I was your age, I thought that anything I wanted bad enough, I could do. *Some days,* some days, I still feel the same way. But most days I don't. "Where there's a will, there's a way," was always my motto. But—I still have the *will,* but I don't seem to be able to find the ways!

I think we've really got to start thinking in terms of not trucking our food nine million miles all over the country. I don't see any reason why Vermont can't produce almost anything it needs. So maybe you won't have a head of iceberg lettuce in February, so what? I don't know, maybe we'll be forced into it, maybe that's the only way it will come about. Maybe there won't be enough gasoline to farm as we do now, and truck things all over. In a way, I *hope* we'll get so damn short of fuel that we'll realize what we're doing! And get the railroads back on the tracks; and in New England, we've got to start trying to produce what we need. New England especially, we're the poop-hole of the world; everything we have comes from somewhere else. Thirty-five per cent of the cost of the concentrates that we feed our cows is *freight.* Here we are with a bumper surplus crop of grain out in the Midwest, farmers sitting on piles of it because they can't make any profit. And by the time it gets to New England, it costs so damn much that we're hurtin. They're hurtin out there, and we are back here, and the transportation companies are the ones making the money. I hope the energy crisis will bring people to their senses. But it will take something like that.

The milk you get back from the store isn't fit to drink. I produce a super product here. We have Jersey cows, we try to be very, very clean, we produce a *good*-tasting milk. And then it gets put in with all the milk that's produced, and they lug it around for two weeks and they put a shelf life of two more weeks on it, and then the American consumer gets it and starts drinking Pepsi-Cola!

It seems impossible to get a premium price for a premium product these days. There's no question in my mind that a bottle of my milk should be worth about twice what a carton of store-bought milk is worth, but the public doesn't recognize this.

I think it keeps coming down to Marie's basic tenet about everything: that it's a matter of education, an education about priorities and what's important. The general public is so ignorant about the problems of agriculture that it's incredible. Just on the most basic level, there are kids that have been born and brought up in *Hinesburg* that can't tell one breed of cattle from another, much less understand the milking process. And the kids from *Burlington,* most of them don't know one end of a cow from another! Starting in kindergarten, an awareness of agriculture should be taught, and I don't mean "Oh look at the poor farmer." I mean *show* them about agriculture from the time they're this big, so that they grow up aware of their dependence and interaction with agriculture. So they won't always have this *adversary* position with farmers.

We have, for the last five or six years, run an apprenticeship program in the summer. They are usually young college students, or people seriously interested in agriculture, or pre-vet students. They get some practical experience here. Most of the agricultural colleges teach you a lot of book learning but you don't ever get to see a cow. We feel there should be more on-the-farm programs like ours; even if all they learn in two and half months is that they *hate* it, it's worth something. But it's surprising how many serious young people have come through here, and how many have gone on too!

I think it's mutually beneficial. Some people would say that we're exploiting the kids because all they get is room and board, but we do have to train them. And we have one of the highest-producing Jersey herds in the whole state, and the cows can't just be handled any old way. It takes time, and there's cost, and so forth. But the kids do two things for us. First, they keep us in contact with young people and what they're thinking about, which is refreshing. And they do provide extra arms and legs.

A lot of them have gone on to really do something in agriculture. And it's so hard for someone who has no experience to get a job, because they have to have experience before they can get a job, so— Marie's always been in teaching and has always liked teaching, and we've always had young people around us some way or other, seems though. Over the years, we've had a lot of young people with problems that have come to us for one reason or another. We've just seemed to collect people, and the farm situation, the farm experience *helps* people, there's just no question about that. There was a spell when you couldn't find any young people that would have anything to do with a farm, and then it turned around again. The last six, seven years there's this whole group of young people that are turned off by other ways of life and we began to get letters, phone calls.

And it has spread some. I think there's a lot more farmers willing to take on, especially women. You know what farmers are learning? That women make awful good milkers, that they make really good cow people. And now you'll even sometimes see old standard farmers advertising for women milkers. There's a young woman out at one of the biggest operations around here doing all the breeding and the book-keeping and everybody says she's doing a bang-up job. I think there is beginning to be a recognition that women are superior around cattle.

Marie: I think that they are not so geared to our highly indus-trialized, highly organized society and do have some more *empathy* with the cattle and you do have to have that to be successful, *really* successful, with cattle.

Marion: It isn't some sentimental thing about "Oh, you cute lit-tle cow," you know. It *isn't* a sentimental, mother response. There's a rapport that a lot of women have—I don't mean all women have it. Men can have it, there are a lot of good cow men, but there are a lot of men that work with cattle all their lives and they don't have the slightest idea about a cow. I know lots of them. For one thing, if a woman is interested, she's not a typical woman in the first place. If she's interested, she's *really* interested. It isn't just another job, a way to make a living. She's really interested in cattle, so you sort of divide out the women anyway. And our experience has been very, very favor-able with women. I'd a lot rather have women milking the cows than men. Of course, I think . . . women are superior to men in lots of ways! There's some things on the farm—I don't mean a woman can't do okay with the field work, the machinery, whatever; I've done it all my life and you *can* do it—but maybe in that area a man can do as well, maybe even better, I don't know. But when it comes to cattle, women have the edge, or sheep, or any livestock.

You can have a real love for the animals, and you'll find yourself drawn to one animal more than another, but it isn't this notion that you're sentimental. It's something else, something deeper than that, something more important.

Marie: You realize that to really work *with* this animal, you've got to understand her and have a sympathy with her. Some kind of insight that lets you see that maybe something's wrong with the cow. Now there's a lot of people that work for you, a lot of men, that don't ever see that.

Marion: Some people could be around animals for thirty years and never would have an eye for them. Others will come along, and they'll walk in the barn and something just won't look right, they'll spot it and do something about it. It's a knack and a feel, and I find more women have it than men. I also find, and that may be because I am a woman, that our women trainees are more responsive to the chance to *learn*. I've got a young man right now that I may have to let go, who knows a tremendous amount for his age but who thinks he knows everything. And I cannot get through to him that there's still a lot for him to learn. And I think that's more apt to be male than female.

I worked on a dairy farm from the time I was thirteen, in summers, and in the summers when I was in college too. There was a small herd of Jerseys though primarily it was a vegetable farm. We sold vegetables in Philadelphia. There was a woman, actually, that owned that farm and ran it. But that's how I first got to know something about cows. I don't suppose I really knew a lot when I started in Connecticut. You're thirteen, fourteen, and you think you really know quite a lot, but you *don't* know quite a lot too. And then when you're on your own, you learn. You learn *fast*. You make a lot of mistakes and have a lot of problems that aren't problems when you know more. We didn't have too many . . . *monstrous* setbacks—

Marie: It's amazing really, I mean I think she must have an innate talent for farming because, *really,* I sometimes look back on it and wonder how we were as successful as we were! Marion learned a lot of things because she *had* to; there was no one else around who was going to do it.

Marion: The nitty-gritty you learn on your own when you go and you have to do something. And most things are fairly simple. Plumbing is a matter of logic; ordinary wiring is also a matter of logic. Most health problems—well, health problems are becoming more sophisticated because of the stress we're putting the animals under, asking them to milk more than they ever were intended to—so health problems are a little more sophisticated. But there's usually only a few things that go wrong with a milking animal: it's usually either reproductive, or in the udder, or in the lungs, oh, and the digestive system.

And, of course, you make a lot of mistakes. You really need to work a farm for three years before you know the land and know the soil. It's a lot of hard work, and you just do what you can do. You get what information you can, but you know, we don't have three books in this house on agriculture. There's just not a lot that's been useful. We depend on a nutritionist with one of the feed companies for a lot of information, and we talk with other farmers, and we have a very good vet who's willing to discuss things. But you do, you just seem through the years to *absorb* pertinent knowledge, and if you have a problem, you sometimes can just pull the solution out of that background of experience.

You might be afraid you're going to do something wrong, and you *do* do some things wrong now and then. I don't think I've ever been responsible for the death of an animal because of gross maltreatment. I've sometimes lost an animal and in thinking back over it, thought what I might have done differently. As far as working the land goes, I never have been into crops as much as I've been into animals. I know the basics about getting the land ready and planting, and so forth, and I guess there's no phase of the operation that I haven't done.

We have had an old man that's worked here several times and the last time he was here, he said, "It's getting so that anything you can't do yourself, maybe you hadn't better do." And I've thought of that so many times because these days we're forced into hiring people to do so many things, and they very seldom do it the way you want it done. And that's a problem all these big operations are getting into too.

Another problem that agriculture has that other businesses don't have is that we work in a peculiar economy: everything we buy, we buy at retail; and everything we sell, we sell at a price which is set for us. We can't survive in that kind of a situation. Granted, we make things worse for ourselves, with heavy indebtedness, heavy rates of interest, destructive farming practices; you can get the tiger by the tail and just can't let go. And the only thing you can do is, you know, just fight against it as best you can. Don't use the pesticides, don't use the herbicides . . . but then, we do use herbicides. I *hate* using herbicides, but I can't pay the minimum wage to someone to cultivate the corn and afford to feed it to cows, with the amount of money they are giving us for our milk. If I could take my costs, like every other industry, and add even ten per cent profit and charge that for my product, *then* I could do some of the things that I know I should do. And I'm sure that this, on a much grander scale, is what a lot of farmers are saying.

In fact, I think that's what we should be screaming about instead of asking for more subsidies and parity. Instead of that business, that was imposed on us also. It's put the farmer in a position where every nickel he wants to get, he has to go beg the government for it. And it's an untenable situation.

We came within an inch of selling all the cows this spring. Oh, I'm not really thinking of going anyplace else. But there's always times you get disgusted with where you are, isn't there? Total discouragement; it just gets to be too much after a while. The older I get, the more permanent the notion gets. It gets harder and harder for me to do all the work, and I really think it gets harder and harder to get good help. I don't think it's just someone over fifty saying, "Things aren't like they used to be!" I don't think they *are*. People just don't produce as much work as they used to. I used to do all that work in that barn there with one other person, and now it takes me at least two others. And it's not only my slowing down, I'm sure. Other jobs are so much easier than farming, it's hard to find people to do it.

It might've been smart to sell the cows this spring with prices so high and keep the young cows and come back into it when they start to milk. But I seem to have a hard time making that kind of decision after so many years.

And the job market for aging overweight farmers is . . . slim. And I don't know that I could set out now to work. We *could* get an awful pile of money if we'd sell the land for development. If we went that route, I probably wouldn't have to worry about what I was going to do, but . . .

A few years ago, we bought a piece of land over on the other side of town; we hayed it, and used the barn, and so forth. And then it looked like a good idea to sell it and consolidate our financing. And we tried and tried to sell it for farmland, but we couldn't do it without knocking the price down so low we'd take an unreasonable loss. So finally we sold it for houses, ten-acre lots for one house, on beautiful hay land. It just tears me up. You know, I'll tell somebody we could probably sell this farm for four or five hundred thousand dollars.

And they'll say, "What's wrong with that?"

But I just can't—I must be *nuts* because all my problems would be solved in a way—but I hate the idea of it. Especially to do that to the home farm. I wouldn't want to stay around here if we did that. This other was bad enough.

I *can* picture myself not getting up at five every morning and working until nine every night, pretty easily. But not farming at all? I don't know . . . no, I don't know . . . I worry that I won't be able to keep on doing the work forever. And the thing is, you'd like to maybe not have to . . . not always work quite so hard. What I *would* like to do is still do some field work and kind of manage the cows, but have some interested people that were into it, that would really work *with* me, to kind of take some of the load off.

The other thing I'm worried about is that the economics of the thing are going to force me out of this kind of farming: bucket milking, individual cow care. You've got to work your butt off and you've got to have more help than a mechanized farm. If I were a family, I could do it. If I had a husband and a couple of interested kids. That's the ideal situation for my kind of farm. It would be a beautiful life, a beautiful place, a beautiful operation, if you had a family that was really interested.

No Time for Paul Newman
Alice Tripp

Alice Tripp is in her late fifties and lives in Belgrade, Minnesota. In the early years of her marriage, she had four children in rapid succession. Then in their mid-thirties, she and her husband, John, gave up city living and moved the family to a farm. Farm work for Alice was a shock, as she rapidly had to master new skills. Ten years later, Alice became an English teacher in the local high school, picking up the career she had trained for but never practiced, and finding some unexpected independence.

In 1976, the local power company decided to build the world's highest-voltage power line across Minnesota, carrying power from the coal fields of North Dakota. The power line follows a curious path, zigzagging to avoid a major corporate farm area and crossing dozens of family farms instead. Alice and John Tripp became involved with their neighbors in a struggle to stop the power line, and eventually Alice ran for governor of Minnesota in 1978. She ran as a protest candidate and polled a respectable percentage of the Democratic vote in a heavily Democratic state.

Alice is alternately merry and pensive, vigorous and somber. She has a breadth of understanding that defies all stereotypes, and a quick wit.

"Well, what do you want to know?" she demanded at my second visit, and then laughed as I stuttered. "Oh, it's nice to turn the tables on you for once!"

We have a two-hundred-and-fifty-acre dairy farm and we milked fifty cows up to last March. We've only been here for twenty-two years, so we're not like most of the people around here. Their fathers and their grandfathers, and maybe even *their* grandfathers, farmed this land. So we always felt a bit like outsiders.

John made the decision to start farming. And I think he made it before he ever told me about it! Because he was a chemical engineer, and every place we lived, he spent a little time looking at farms. Then finally, the FHA said, "Why don't you go to Minnesota, farms are bigger and the loans are better." And since we were from Minnesota originally, that appealed to us, and so he quit his job and we came here. We'd looked for quite a few years—Maryland, Michigan, Minnesota.

He'd told me, "Now we might not have indoor plumbing, but we sure are going to have good land!" And he worked with soil maps, that's how we found this farm. And we were lucky to find it, because around here, farms go to neighbors. Now we've already got lots of neighbors, considering the fact that we're getting to retirement age, who are looking to buy our farm for their sons. It's a very stable community, farming is very much respected here. Farms are very prosperous, through here.

John says that he's a conservative. He's *not* an organization person. That's why he's here, he didn't want to work for a company. He's not a joiner, cause he doesn't like to go to meetings where people all do the same thing. So he's really not a conventional heel-the-line person, you know. That's why we're on the farm, and I imagine that's why many people are on the farm. A lot of people have come back from the cities to lead their own lives, be able to direct their own life. And that's one thing that we've got to protect, is that *possibility* of having a farm where you can do that. I think there's a grave danger of that going, too. *Time* magazine's now saying that the only farms that are going to last are those that are big enough to be efficient, run by computers, that sort of thing. I believe, myself, that the family farm is most efficient, and that it's *important,* because it develops personal potential.

Well now, when we came out here the kids and I and John, all of us, had to learn from the beginning. None of us knew anything about farming, we didn't even know what the machinery was for! We went out to the barn with stopwatches and clipboards and milked the cows that way. We quickly expanded, got more cows, and in a very few years got rid of our chickens and hogs, to simplify our operation. This farm is a balanced operation, we use all our crops to feed our own fifty-cow herd.

But coming to the problems of making the farm work for us, these were terrific. And I think that we succeeded, because we kept our heads above water and got the kids through school all right. But they had to go on scholarship. We never had any CASH.

I remember somebody asked John after we'd been here for a year if he ever missed the city, and he said, "Well, the only thing I miss is the dirty, filthy, smoky money."

Because it was pretty hard going. When you're working that hard, you don't question whether you're doing the right thing, you just know you are. I remember the first year during haying time, we felt like our eyes were *bleeding,* we were so tired. And John and I, our hands swelled and we couldn't sleep at night because they hurt so. We'd never handled hay bales before, or milked cows, or handled all that heavy stuff. The kids had never done anything but make their beds before we came. But they're good kids and they knew they had to work. Of course, they immediately *quit* making their beds when they got here!

Some of the things that happened were kind of interesting because—I've found out *since* that farm kids get up before school and do chores. Ours didn't. I helped with chores in the morning, and they did them at night. Then they'd come in at night and want to read the paper or do their homework, and John would come in and say, "It's a *Panic* Situation!" And we'd all bail out. I suppose there were times they resented it, but they have a lot of respect for the farm, for farming, for the land, and they really loved it. They truly did.

We knew so little in those days, that John sent Mike over to dig up the neighbor's oats and see if they were sprouting faster than ours! And once Christy, she's our oldest, was reading a book on having healthy stock.

"You know what?" she said. "The pigs are supposed to have curly tails."

So we all rushed out to the barn to see if they did! We were very, very green. It's kind of a miracle that we made it, I guess.

I told my husband when we came to the farm, "You really will have to have *some* respect for my routine!"

One day I was ironing and John came in just spitting, "I hope you're enjoying the ironing, cows are out all over the place and I just can't get them in!"

Well, *that* was the last time I ever ironed anything! You need two people for so *many* jobs on a farm; and when the kids were in school, I had to be available. I wasn't always cheerful about it, though. Sometimes I was so mad because I couldn't . . . and John said, "NO MORE BAKING BREAD! There's always bread in the oven when I want you to come outside!" So . . . I wasn't always as helpful as I could have been. I did have a routine, I didn't wash clothes on Monday, iron on Tuesday or anything like that. But I got frustrated when I always had to go outside and couldn't even get the dishes done. It would have been nice if I'd known a little more what I was getting into. Really inquired, known a few more farm women, known how hard they worked.

One day when I first came here, I went to buy some chickens from Ruthie Turk, who I didn't know. Ruthie Turk is a beautiful girl, woman, and wore beautiful clothes and I always thought she was some kind of a *queen*. Anyway, she was out in the barn and she was throwing all the loose bales of hay up to the loft. Her husband did the tied-up bales because they were easier. I was astonished at that. There she looked like she just stepped out of the beauty parlor and she's doing at least half the farm work! Then she works at the bar in town at night too—a lot of women around here do that—on Fridays and Saturdays. It was just astonishing to me . . . and I wasn't *quite* as jealous of Ruthie after that!

And the REAL revelation to me was to see how hard the women worked on these farms. I didn't run the tractors very much. The boys had to do that, and that was revelation for them, learning to run the tractors. Our oldest daughter also learned to run a tractor, but the real heavy work, the boys did. She had to pick up and wash eggs, run the tractor some, but the boys got to do the plowing until they left. THEN *we* had to learn to plow!

And one time when I was plowing—we have a problem here because our season's short and we often have to plow in cold weather. And that time it was *so* hard and cold, and my stops were sticking. I was turning up huge clods and my rows weren't straight.

And Mike came home from school, and he said, "Mother, you've *ruined* the poor land!"

The field work, that's the real fun work. When you get stuck in the barn that's not so much fun for most people, I think. On the other hand, the women out here *all* of them milk and plow. They even have plowing contests for women. And they also are big partners in the decisions that get made. There's no question of the husband's business not being the woman's business. On the other hand, they go to meetings with their husbands and—well, they never have before spoken up as much as they did on the power line. On the power line, the women suddenly really spoke up. Now, people have told me that the women around here have always been pretty feisty, pretty independent and outspoken. Maybe the women around here are at home, but in public, I don't see that as much around here as in the next county. But boy, the women sure carry their share of the load! The difference, I think, is that this area where I live is solid German Catholic, very big families. Very, well, "man rules the world" kind of thing, is what they're told in church. Whereas Pope County is Scandinavian, Protestant, I think it makes a difference. The women down here, I think, probably have as much to say about their own farms as the men do, but in public they don't speak up. For instance, they're not going to vote for the ERA, that sort of thing. But when it comes to the home, they have power. We had a judge once who came out to speak to our 4-H and said, "You people don't know how lucky you are to be needed." And the women out here know that they are *needed,* that their work is very important. They don't just have coffee klatches out here.

And I think that's very important for the kids too, they have a real feeling for their own worth. I also think they work too hard, I think they don't have enough time to themselves. The work ethic is so strong here that they don't enjoy idleness. What are they going to do when they grow up? That bothers me a bit. But my kids manage to enjoy idleness so much they don't even care if they have a job!

I would guess that marriages on the farm last longer because women have so much more part in what's going on, making decisions, financial decisions. There's still a lot of macho, "I am the boss" thing. But at the same time, women get told, and usually consulted, about everything. And boy, they work hard enough that they ought to have a lot to say about decisions! They're out in the fields and in the barns. And for that reason, couples may have ties that other people don't have, and they may know each other better. They also don't have *time* to go out and find themselves another place to go, someone to run around with. I sure haven't. I *never'd* have time for Paul Newman!

I think being married is a pretty good deal. *John* thinks it's absolutely essential to a woman's happiness to be married. He was all for his daughters getting married. I don't know why. Oh, I guess he doesn't like the idea of living alone. I think some people enjoy living alone, some people do better living alone. Of course, there are also a lot of lonely people in the world, but marriage probably isn't the solution. I think having better communities is important, to be able to mix with people. I go to church sometimes, and I'll tell you the truth, I often go just to be around other people, to be part of a group of people. Now when I take Meggie to church—she agreed to go with me one time at Christmastime—and *right* in the middle of the service, she got up and walked out.

"They aren't there because they want to be there, Mother," she said, "they're there because they think they have to be."

Who's she to go passing judgment on everyone? You go passing judgment about their customs, and the narrowness of their lives, and how they do what somebody else tells them to, but maybe they're *happier* doing it that way. Traditions are set for them and they feel they are part of a community because they are part of a tradition that's important to them. They'd be lonely without that feeling of belonging. We never really felt we belonged to this community and I don't guess we ever would.

But it's been a good life. Farming is a good way of life, though I will reserve my judgment and say that you can't do that much to the kids and expect them to go to school. It's too much, and they do work too hard and something happens. The kids begin to resent that, then when they get into high school, the parents are bribing them to stay. And some of the kids are turning against the farms. But they go to the city and quickly find out they'd rather be back on the farms. In this state, we have the weekend exodus, everybody in Minneapolis leaves on Friday and goes *home*.

This is actually a pretty invigorating place to live. Especially now, now with the power line struggle we see a lot of young people from the cities; they're always up here now. And our neighbors. We have met just *terrrriffic* people on the power line struggle. It's broadened our whole—*everybody's*—horizons tremendously. Because we worked on a farm in this community, went to church in this community, went to school in this community, we know how parochial life can be. Well, in a struggle, you meet other people, realize others have that same struggle, you talk, become outgoing, you *have* to.

It is remarkable now after three years how many people are still coming to meetings and still interested and active. There are some who have given up, but really it is remarkable how many have stayed for so long. And it's people of all ages. Many of them are older than us, family people, farm people.

When it all started I was teaching high school and I didn't go to the meetings. My teacher friend wanted me to go and I should have, but I didn't. Well, John went to several meetings and he was always a spectator and didn't speak up much.

So finally, April thirteenth, nineteen seventy-six, he said, "You have to come and talk for me."

And I said, "No, I have to correct papers. I'm an English teacher!"

But I went and I was just astonished at what people were saying and doing, and at the way they were treated. Neighbors who had never talked to very many people were standing up and talking about what was happening to them, expressing their fears about this technology that they didn't understand but they knew was wrong. And people from the state, along with power company owners, sat there absolutely bored and cynical.

Anyway, by the time it was my turn to talk, I was so angry I could hardly talk. And afterwards, John talked. And once we got started, we never stopped. We quickly got involved in talking a lot and running a telephone tree, and getting meetings going. June of seventy-six, we found out the power line was coming onto our land. It's too bad that that makes you more involved than ever, too bad that you can't be involved for other people as much as you are for yourself.

As John told me after that first meeting, "It's going to be the biggest power line in the world, and our farmers don't want the biggest *anything* in the world on their land."

And these farmers are prosperous enough that they don't need the money, have never been interested in the money. And they haven't picked up their money from the power company yet. They could have a long time ago. At one meeting early on, Governor Anderson's aides spent the whole day trying to get John and the other farmers who were there to name a price.

"How much do we have to pay you guys?" they kept asking.

And at a meeting in the western part of the state, one of the local power coop directors kept asking "What's your price?" and no one would name a price. And you know what he said up there? He said, "You must have some syndicate behind you."

And somebody else from the government said to me once, "Who's organizing you people?"

The farmers around here are prosperous, and they're very, very conscious of the value of their land; they just won't sell it. Well, we started organizing and there happened to be a couple of very good organizers. It's been a very spontaneous group. Nonprofessional, but very effective. And at times we had *everybody* in this area on our side. CURE was the first group that formed and they had quite a widespread reputation. But what happened was that they had a board of directors, and the leader of it didn't meet with the people very much. So then at each meeting and at each different place new leaders began to emerge. So you could also say that after that, there were no leaders.

Then in the fall of nineteen seventy-six, we had these confrontations on Constitution Hill, and people were so ingenious at stopping the company's surveyors. All of us would drive clear up there, thirty-five miles, every morning. The first morning, we had huge tractors and trucks in front of the surveyors' platforms. And we had coffee and sandwiches and cookies. The second day we brought out chain saws so the surveyors couldn't communicate. So that day, the surveyors just went home. And the next day we got permission from the town board to dig up the road. Now, this was wintertime and the fellas were out there all night with their diggers making holes. When the surveyors came in the morning, there was a sign "Road Under Construction." By that time, some of the highway patrol were involved and one of them came over and knocked down the construction sign.

So one of us said, "Now look here, the town board said we could do that and you'd better put that sign back."

So, he went back to his radio and called the town board, and they said, "Yes, indeed, there's road construction out there."

So then they tried to read us a court order over the bullhorn, so we all began to sing loud enough so we couldn't hear the bullhorn. The judge sent out three different court orders trying to get the people to quit up there, and none of them ever got read.

All our tactics were purely spontaneous, and very ingenious. We were having a lot of fun then, though there'd already been some legal battles. One farmer was under court order not to appear out there, because he'd started the whole thing by pushing the surveyors' transit over with his tractor when they were out at his place. So we were already becoming acquainted with the courts. Then finally, one by one, we were hauled off in the cars and they read the court orders to us. But because of that action up there, we delayed them for many, many months. We took our case clear to the state Supreme Court, and lost there. We've had many processions down to the city, we've filled the state capitol and stopped business down there. We'd got sort of a network going where we'd call people from different places and say "Come," for a meeting or a demonstration, and they'd come.

I'd never been an activist before the power line came along. Oh, I'd been involved in a couple little things, like when two teachers got fired, I objected to the way they were fired. You might say I've been a little bit of a minor troublemaker. I don't like to go along with the establishment, or the school principal, or whoever, just because they say it's so. I like to do what I think is right. I got mad at the bishop because the only space he gave the Berrigan brothers was on the back page of the diocese paper and I told him I'd drop the paper. But that's about the extent of my radicalism.

I don't know if I was ever a real iconoclast, but I *resented* establishment procedures in school, you know! I'll tell you, this is what happened one time, we had an award for boys. A boy, a basketball player, had been killed, and there was an award for a boy every year in his name. Without even thinking about it, it went on for a couple years.

And finally one of the younger teachers said, "Well, why don't we have an award for women?"

So I started agitating and talking to people about women. I went downtown and talked to a woman who was part of a women's club to see if they wouldn't like to sponsor an award. And the principal came by as I was talking to her and said, "*What* are you up to now?"

And we really had to *fight* to get that women's award!

The men said, "You have to have somebody who's gotten killed before you can do that!"

And it never had the prestige of the other one, but we did finally get it through. They were so threatened by the fact that women, girls, might have an award! *That* was being radical!

So anyway, when the power company surveyors came here to Stearns County, we plotted and plotted how to stop them. When they saw the resistance, they didn't even get out of their cars. They just went to another county. But wherever they were, we kept it up, and kept it up. That was the first action to try and stop the surveyors from laying out the power line.

Then people that had been more active and knew more about protest movements said that we've got to have some arrests to test the laws. Voluntary arrests. And we got bolder, and bolder, and got arrested. But somehow I never *voluntarily* got arrested! I was arrested three times but none of them was voluntary, each time I was doing very innocent things. Once, I was standing by a transit talking to a power line worker trying to tell him that in California they call this an eight hundred KV line; and I went back to the car to get a piece of paper to show him, and when I came back, I was arrested. Obstructing legal process. And another time they used an injunction against us, but the judge ruled that the injunction was only valid against the person named.

They stopped us on our own lane, in our own fields. Once they brought out over two hundred highway patrol. When the state brings out two hundred highway patrol to deal with a few farmers, your respect for law just diminishes. Many days, there were more highway patrol than protesters. Half of all the patrol in the whole state was over here! Not only that, but they had two helicopters and an airplane and they did this constant surveillance, which was pretty dramatic. I think a lot of people became very cynical about government seeing how a state police force can be used by a private company that way, and become just a goon squad, really, for the company. It had never happened to us before. I think anybody, even the most conservative of people, couldn't see the police being used that way and not take action, at least take a stand of some kind.

People that were most involved in the protest actions became new leaders. And in a way I suppose there were two of us, two women, running a lot of things, but then lots of people were always involved. Me and Gloria Voida were just gabby, I guess; we liked to speak a lot. There were other people who were willing to take their turns at meetings and hearings. But if there wasn't, Gloria and I were always willing to fill in the gap. We had very informal meetings. Being informal, the responsibility never weighs too heavily on any one person.

When we brought up the question of the esthetics of the power line, how those poles look marching across your field, the director of the state Pollution Control Agency said, "We have no esthetic standards." No esthetic standards, so we can't use that, we can't talk about esthetics.

And, really, esthetics is a strange one for farmers to talk in public about. But one time on the radio, oh, early in the campaign, one of our neighbors that already had a small power line spoke, he had a German accent, he said, "I haf to sit here, I can *hear* dat power line. Now vhat's going to happen vhen one dat's five times dat big comes?" And, indeed, that five times as big one came and his land was a corner, so that it crosses it in two directions. And that family was so proud of their view, and so concerned about the way the farm looks. The soil is *taken care of* and everything's in good repair, and the animals have a good habitat. And then somebody comes along with the power to say, "We're going to put this right here, anyhow."

I think farm people are very aware of the *quality* of life that is affected by the power line, not only the way it looks but what it represents. Now they've found out that they actually do get headaches when the line's on, and some people have broken out in rashes. There are real health considerations and we're still expected to just accept it. The thing that got aired a lot was health and safety, which is harder to prove, though it's easier to talk about. You know, you can't talk about esthetics. But you *can* talk about your TV being knocked out or your CB radio, or the pacemaker in your heart.

So, we get ignored. And the residue is some *very* angry people. Angry at the government, angry at the corporation's control. The government allowed the corporation to move in, and the corporation *used* the government. The governor, the state agencies, even the legislature were used by the power companies over and over again. And they are still being used, not only by the power company but by every other company powerful enough to hire some permanent lobbyists. People are not only angry, but they are beginning to know some things about how things happen, and to look at what happens next. If they're angry enough to take down a power line tower, they're pretty mad. Or even to shoot out an insulator.

They're angry and they're disillusioned, and the fact that they're still determined is the best thing. They still have interest, they're still talking about it, and they're going to fight it one way or another. I hope it leads to people being *involved* in broader issues. Some people say about other groups, "You never did anything for us, why should we help you?" But there's lots of other people talking about going to the Black Hills for an Indian pow-wow, and will contribute to something like that. And they went all the way to Nebraska to help out with a power line struggle there.

I just wrote to my sister and I said, "I don't know, I'm a little worried that it might be egotism to think that just by going to a meeting you can affect change." So sometimes I wonder a little bit about being an activist or running off to a lot of meetings. You know, maybe I'm just a gadfly that's not going to accomplish anything. What happens is that I've had to turn down some family affairs, and the next two weekends I've got some *conflicts* and I've got to make some decisions. And sometimes I think it's a little egotistical, I'm not so sure what I can do, that I'm so effective. One more body, I guess. Sometimes John thinks we've got to quit. And our son, one of our sons, tells us we've got to think about quitting this power line activity. And John doesn't see us getting into anything else because we never did before.

But it doesn't appear to me that it's the *time* to quit yet . . . Actually, I should tell you that we did a little work for the Republican party at one time. And when we came here, we offered to work for the Republican party. And they didn't accept our offer, we were aliens. I don't think we'd fit in very well now!

Running for governor was a lot of fun. I made some really good friends. The people who campaigned with me are *really* good friends. And I picked up some more concern for people. I realized how many people there are that feel like they've been trampled on, that don't have a spokesman, that don't even know where to turn. The people in the Boundary Waters area were feeling like they've been just absolutely ignored. And the labor people, I'd never had much contact with labor, and I really have a lot of respect for them. That's the main thing it did, was give me contact with people. And the lesbians in Minneapolis were among the nicest people I know. My daughter and I went to one of the lesbian meetings, and *moving* . . . gee. And racial minorities, were also an important connection. So, you—you broadened your horizons. As a teacher, I had to . . ˙. I did have always a kind of broad-minded attitude about *tolerating* people. I've had to defend homosexuality to students who didn't know anything about it, and welfare to students who don't think anyone should be on welfare, so . . . but I didn't exactly *know*. It was a kind of theoretical thing, I hadn't met people, and now I've kind of really opened my eyes.

I had always considered myself a Republican. But with Nixon, I suppose that nobody wanted to be a Republican after that. But . . . I was only *kind* of a Republican. John always accused me of being a parlor pink. I never was as conservative as he was. Now we've *both* been radicalized, and sometimes he will admit it more than others. But we've both been through a change, and that's happened to a lot of other people here too.

John is very broad-minded and very tolerant; he taught me a lot about being broad-minded. He doesn't want to see anyone hurt, ever. Sometimes he doesn't sound that way, but—so you don't *really* know how people feel. I think that there are people around here who are like that, people who are more tolerant than you would ever guess.

We don't know people very well, really. And when they have an issue, they will speak up on that issue. They'll speak out for the rights of individuals and American people to determine their own lives. They feel that in our system we *do* have the right of individual self-determination. And in the power line struggle we all spoke up for it. But I'm very much afraid we don't have it anymore. I'm pretty cynical really, about all that; that's why I'm not very much interested in traditional politics.

What the power line struggle did was to give us the feeling that we might be doing some good. We both thought that we should do *everything* we could to help people, even what looked like a futile gesture, because it *might* help and we should get people involved. That wasn't a future thing, it was just a right-now action thing. You have to live from day to day when you're going through a crisis like that. But as far as planning for the future, John and I are beginning *now* instead of ten years ago. I don't know, sometimes plans don't work out. But I think we didn't want to face that someday we'd be retiring.

I kept saying to John, "We've got to make some plans."

And he'd say, "I'd rather sit still."

I envy people who say, "I know this is the right thing to do," and then go do it. They're so smart. How come they're so smart? *They* would know whether to rent the farm out or whether to sell the farm, and do it. Just because I have this romantic notion about wanting to live here, well that's hardly enough reason to stay. On the other hand, what other reason is there? I'm sorry none of the kids want the farm. I think it's a really good life. And it's a good way to get a start, through your family, the only way now. It would be nice to have it in the family. But . . . they like the city.

John made out a scenario the other day for me: we'd spend the summer in Minnesota, FALL in Illinois, of all places! What's in Illinois? Winter in TEXAS! We don't know anybody in TEXAS. I don't know . . . we do want to get away from the terrible winters in Minnesota. But you have to be *doing* something. I just don't know what yet. Carpenters make sixteen dollars an hour! Wish we weren't such *lousy* carpenters! It's not good, I don't think just to live—maybe you *have* to live just day-to-day, I've got *plenty* to do if I think about it—but you can't just hang on to that, I think you need something more. You have to occupy yourself. I have a sister who was an M.D. and now she runs a nursery school full time, and she's seventy.

I think . . . I think I would like to work with senior citizens. Course being a senior citizen, they may not be so anxious to have me, but I'd like to. I'm thinking about retirement-home senior citizens, they're so *bored*. I've always wanted to get into adult teaching. I have these dreams. Seattle had a great thing, at the Seattle Center there's this big building and they have dances. We were there on Valentine's Day and everyone was wearing red and white. LONG dresses, red *blazers,* having a great time. That old-time music, dancing away. Big band playing all the old favorites. It was really great. John wouldn't even get on the floor. I *also* have a dream of dancing!

John resists nostalgia. He doesn't like to go back home, to where we grew up, and he doesn't like to visit old friends. Me, I like a little nostalgia. I'm a real rememberer. I don't want to leave the farm. But it's been a very hard year for John. He doesn't have the equipment and he's getting weaker. He's not strong and really . . . well, I had to hold the wrench and listen to him cuss. It's hard for him. Now, though, he's getting kind of interested in soybeans, and I think that would be fun.

John is more worried about money than me. I figure, what the heck, I'll just go live with my doctor son!

Fifty, maybe fortyish, not too long ago, I began to really *enjoy* life. I decided, well what the heck, I've worried all these years about money and I'm *not* going to worry about money anymore. That's enough of that! And I don't worry about the kids. The kids . . . you can suffer with them, but you can't change anything . . . but I don't think the kids leaving caused me to stop worrying—my kids never *quite* grew up. They never *quite* got over the hump! I don't know . . . after I started teaching—at first, I didn't think about this much—but after I was teaching for a couple years, I said to myself, "I really don't have to worry about whether I can afford to buy oranges this week. I am teaching and I get to make a *few* decisions for myself."

John was very uptight when we were first married and I had to write down *everything* I spent. That was how we did the budget, I just wrote down everything I spent; no planning, just everything I spent. And by that time, I was pregnant and the doctor wanted to know everything I *ate*. So if I so much as got a Hershey Bar, both John and the doctor would get me! It's hard being married and being pregnant right away. I guess it would have been even harder if I wasn't pregnant, though, because I was very lonely and he wouldn't let me work then. I loved to arrange flowers and got a job in a flower shop, and he wouldn't let me work there.

"I am the provider, I've got to be the provider," he said.

All we had was a little apartment and we didn't know anybody— *such* a home for my place to be in! But after I'd been teaching awhile, I began to feel, "Well, yes, I should be a little more independent."

Looking back, I wish I had had the capacity when I was younger for enjoying life and relaxing as much as I do *now*. But you might not be able to achieve that before you get to be fifty. I think about getting older. I will be really upset when I'm not able to type, because the arthritis seems to be settling in my hands. I worry a little bit about that. I can remember when my mother couldn't knit anymore, arthritis runs in the family. And I remember as I got older, *feeling* different parts of my body, and thinking, "Gee, *that* never bothered me before." Because I was a real active person when I was young, you know, and I thought if I didn't go for a long walk at least once a day, well, the sky would fall in. And I was healthy always. That's the only thing that bothers me, arthritis. I suppose there *might* come a time in my life when I'd rather sit still than *not* sit still. But I don't know, there might *not!* Actually, I think the ability to sit still is an enviable thing. Serenity is an admirable quality to me . . . I just don't know if I'll achieve that one!